Helping the Bereaved

Richard S. Dunlop, Ed.D.
University of Missouri–Kansas City

The Charles Press Publishers, Inc.
Bowie, Maryland 20715

Helping the Bereaved

Executive Producer: William L. Gibson
Production Editors: Charlett Bundy; Marlise Reidenbach
Cover Design: Laura Lammens

Library of Congress Cataloging in Publication Data
Dunlop, Richard S.
    Helping the bereaved.
    Bibliography: p.
    Includes index.
    1. Bereavement—Psychological aspects. 2. Grief.
3. Death—Psychological aspects. I. Title.
BF575.G7D86   155.9'37   78-13534
ISBN 0-913486-91-4

Prentice-Hall International, Inc., London
Prentice-Hall of Australia, Pty., Ltd., Sydney
Prentice-Hall of India Private Limited, New Delhi
Prentice-Hall of Japan, Inc., Tokyo
Prentice-Hall of Southeast Asia Pte. Ltd., Singapore
Whitehall Books, Limited, Wellington, New Zealand
Printed in the United States of America

78 79 80 81 82 83 10 9 8 7 6 5 4 3 2 1

ᘓᕊᘓᕊᘓᕊᘓᕊᘓᕊ

CONTENTS

ᘓᕊᘓᕊᘓᕊᘓᕊᘓᕊ

ೲೲೲೲ

PREFACE

ೲೲೲೲ

A task of the educator is to collect that which is known or believed to be true and to "package" that information in a useful way. A task of the psychologist is to apply what is known of people in general to a person in particular, in order to help that person with difficulties which he is having and which are very special to him. Those are two goals of this book. The intent here is to provide information on what is now known about the psychology of dying, death, and especially about bereavement. Secondly, recognizing that nothing can now be done to make bereavement pleasant or comfortable, to describe what mental health professionals and others can do to help those who are in grief to deal most effectively with their great sorrow and to survive it with hope and without undesirable psychological artifacts which can be detrimental in the long term.

Even given the researcher's objectivity and the clear need for mental health professionals and other caring persons to know about the grief syndrome, it takes a certain presumptuousness to write of topics as awesome as these. Still, for years, some person or another has been trying. One of the earliest, probably, was the poet of ancient Egypt who said, "Lo, no man taketh his goods with him." Solomon liked the lyric so well that he put it in Ecclesiastes (5:15); the Greek poet Theognis used it later, five centuries before the Christian era; and Paul was sufficiently enamored of the thought to dictate it for inclusion in the New Testament (I Timothy 6:7). Eventually, the idea wound up in the *Book of Common Prayer*, and ultimately it found its way to the world's theatrical stage as the title of a sparkling Kaufman and Hart comedy of the mid-1930s. This is how our collective wisdom is shaped. Someone writes an impression or an observation; others write it again; many read and consider; and ultimately we have folk dogma: you can't take it with you.

Many other ideas about dying, death, and bereavement have been developing across the centuries. There has been in recent years a particular interest in dying itself, and scholarly research into this mystery has begun, research called *thanatology*. Relatively less has been done with *lamentology*, the study of bereavement, of how best to help grieving persons to contend effectively with that very deep sorrow which, at one time or another, all of us know. So that is what the present book tries to do, despite the unhappiness inherent in such a topic: it attempts to pull together much of what the principal scientific theorists, observers, practitioners of the mental and physical health sciences, and researchers have had to say about the bereavement phenomenon, and to present their beliefs and findings in a way which should prove helpful to the variety of professionals who work with people and their difficulties, and to all of the many deeply concerned others who have family and friends who someday will require special caring and knowledgeable understanding as they work their ways through bereavement.

Few new ideas will be found here. The purposes have been simply to collect knowledge of dying, death, and bereavement, as best we now possess such knowledge, and to present that knowledge in a way which the author hopes will prove useful.

The Bibliography follows the list of references cited throughout the text. Librarians are almost always helpful in locating cited materials for persons who are uncomfortable with library research procedures. Pains have been taken to attribute the sources of knowledge and opinion responsibly and accurately, but if carelessness or oversight have interfered with appropriate attribution, apologies are offered by the present author in advance and with regret.

It should be noted that this is not a book for persons who are now experiencing grief. Those who have recently known the death of some loved person will find much of this book too clinical, too blunt, and far too detached and objective to be of any particular assistance. Bereaved persons don't need to attend clinically to intellectualisms and the findings of research—under the circumstances of mourning, such behavior is only another kind of avoidance and denial. Bereaved persons need mostly to acknowledge their own feelings, to hear their own feelings, to communicate those feelings as best they are able, to others who can share. Perhaps later they might turn here to acquaint themselves with how they might better understand the bereavements of others in order to help them—as well as to understand themselves more fully when the next grief comes, as it inevitably will.

ოოოოო

ACKNOWLEDGMENTS

ოოოოო

Many persons have contributed to the development of this manuscript. Particular recognition is due a few, especially those graduate counselors who have studied bereavement therapies at the University of Missouri-Kansas City. They used early versions of this book in their preparation and added substantially and invaluably to its content and to the quality of its rendering. Of them, the author wishes especially to acknowledge the contributions of Kathryn Jackson and Gale Hofmann who served, respectively, as academic editor and as supplementary research assistant.

Special acknowledgment is extended also to the various publishers who have generously permitted reuse of considerable research and opinion originally printed elsewhere.

Richard S. Dunlop, Ed.D.
Kansas City, Missouri

THE AUTHOR

Dr. Richard S. Dunlop is a psychologist and professor in the School of Education at the University of Missouri-Kansas City, where his work has included the training of professional counselors and psychologists, many of them in the special area of bereavement therapy. This book evolved from his research and lectures in lamentology, and from the research contributions of several collaborating graduate students. The author of various other books and of numerous articles in several aspects of professional counseling and therapeutic psychology, Dr. Dunlop holds degrees from San Diego State University and Arizona State University.

I

DYING

Early American Indians shot arrows into the air to drive away evil spirits; in contemporary military funerals guns are fired at the sky. In modern-day civilian funerals we hurl prayers toward the heavens, as indeed we do as children when our parents teach us to implore the Lord our souls to take if we should die before we wake.

It seems that the fear of death is universally human. The anthropologist Ernest Becker (1) believes it's not only universal but a fundamental motivator of behavior. And if we know that we can't keep death away, we seem at least to insist on keeping it at bay.

> *O death, where is thy sting-a-ling-a-ling,*
> *O Grave, thy victoree?*
> *The bells of hell go ting-a-ling-a-ling*
> *For you but not for me!*
> > *BRITISH MILITARY BALLAD*
> > *WORLD WAR I*

Nonetheless, deaths will happen—about two million a year in the United States alone (2)—and griefs will follow

1

as people experience bereavement. That observation is as real as the observation that the grief process is like many other aspects of human behavior: it is capable of description and study. It's to be hoped that if we can take some time while we are not ourselves involved in a grief reaction to study the phenomenon and understand it, we will be better able to help others more fully when the opportunities next arise—and they will—and perhaps to help ourselves when the next time comes for us to experience our own grief—as that time, too, will come.

Thanatology is the study of dying and death, and more work has been done in researching problems of the dying than on problems of those who live on. The reason is simple enough: a dying person can be studied tactfully. Meticulous records can be kept of his physiological processes which can be measured. Observations may be made of what the person says, what he does, and so on. But as we begin a study which we might call *lamentology*, we find it is virtually impossible to study bereaved persons in the ways which are so relatively convenient to thanatologists. Aldous Huxley remarked in *Eyeless in Gaza* that, "Death is the only thing we haven't succeeded in completely vulgarizing," and he may have been right. Yet, if we are going to understand something of how to help persons live more comfortably with their grief, we have to start somewhere. Perhaps if our purposes are sufficiently innocent, the vulgarity of inquiry will be forgiven.

Probably the best place to start is with the dying person himself. We sometimes overlook it in our preoccupation at a time of death with our own reactions, but let's remember that the dying person has his own grieving to do. That is important: *the dying person has his own grieving to do.* We should remember, too, that the dying person is not just losing himself (which is a considerable loss that other grievers are not having to deal with), but the dying person is also about to lose everything which is important and everyone who is significant to him and whom he loves.

It has been noticed that some dying patients have a compulsive fascination with time—fingering their watches, having several clocks around the room—so if our own grief at the impending loss of some loved person is profound, we must think of what it must be for those who are dying, for whom *every single thing in the whole wide world is about to end*, and *too soon*.

So these discussions will begin with the matter of what happens with dying people. Our attention will go first to the question of whether or not these patients should be told that they are dying.

TELLING THE PERSON

The term *confrontation* refers to the time when the physician tells the patient he has a terminal illness. But confrontation with the dying person doesn't always happen. One study revealed that 12 per cent of Philadelphia physicians—presumably a representative sample—would *never* tell a patient he was dying, and 57 per cent *usually would not* tell; 28 per cent *sometimes* told, and only 3 per cent *usually* did. The questionnaire study included 444 physicians. In another investigation, 88 per cent of physicians at a Chicago hospital reported that it was their policy not to tell persons if they had malignant diseases. "The modal policy is to tell as little as possible in the most general terms consistent with maintaining the cooperation of the patient in treatment" (3).

More often, confrontation refers to the time when the physician tells some member of the patient's family, or the family group, that death can be expected. (Engel recommended in 1964 that news of impending death is best presented in a family group, rather than to some individual member, and in a private setting. It is often desirable, he said, for the person who will take on the task of confrontation to identify in advance some member of the family or constellation of friends whose relation vis-à-vis the dying patient is such that he will be able to retain the composure and judgment necessary to help the more stricken survivors.)

Parkes (4) has pointed out that when physicians disclose bad news they often employ hushed tones, as if in this way they can somehow "minimize the mutilation." But whether the physician whispers, shakes his head, or shouts, it is normally the wife or husband (or perhaps one of the parents) who gets the word first, and that person is faced with a decision which has to be made—sometimes immediately, but certainly before too much time passes: How much of this do we tell the rest of the family? How much do we tell the children, and how? And more importantly: How much of this do we tell the person we love, whom we have learned is not only terribly ill (as we perhaps suspected) but who is, in fact, dying?

The decision is not easily made, not always because of concern for the dying person, but because some people respond with acute grief reactions to the presentation of diagnoses of fatal illnesses (5, 6). In these circumstances, their own psychological responses must be contended with before any thought can be given to the needs of the dying person himself. According to Gullo (7), the initial responses of wives to news of their husbands' life-threatening illness include depression, anxiety, feelings of inadequacy, and role disorder. These sensations are reported as being more pronounced early in the anticipatory process rather than later.

Parkes (8) has observed that many people who find themselves in terminal illness environments (hospitals or nursing homes in about two thirds of these [9]) seem to play down the gravity of circumstances with themselves, friends and relatives, and with the dying patient. Parkes has called this a "gentle deception" carried out with the terminally ill. Perhaps it is done out of belief that if the dying person were told he was dying, he would become depressed and despondent—though in time he will be both, and *must* be both if his dying is to have some psychological comfort to it. However, in an effort to keep the dying person from depression and despondency, the wife puts on a "brave face" and undertakes to communicate to her dying husband that he is going to be all right. Perhaps she half convinces herself, as well. If a surviving wife can achieve an attitude of imagining everything is going to be all right, then she can mislead her dying husband without feeling guilty. Presumably, the patient then dies without knowing that he is dying, and he is altogether more comfortable in the exercise. But, as Parkes points out, the problem is that this kind of deception does not always end with the death.

It is probably true that the major contemporary observer with interest in problems of the dying person is Elisabeth Kubler-Ross, whose books *On Death and Dying* (1970) and *Death: the Final Stage of Growth* (1975) should be read carefully by anyone who works with dying people (10). Kubler-Ross' work concerns itself largely with difficulties of the dying, and, in the main, with prolonged dying from cancer. For the most part, she avoids describing patient experiences in other kinds of dying: myocardial infarction, gross trauma, debilitation from old age, cardiovascular breakdown, and so on. Glaser and Strauss (11) have referred to the time needed to die from varying ailments as "dying trajectories," which range from several months in a cancer ward, to an hour or a few days in an infant care center, to perhaps 10 days in intensive care situations. Clearly there are a variety of time dimensions in dying, the implications of which for emotional helpers have not yet really been explored. Sudden deaths, as an example, appear to be particularly distressing to nurses, who respond to them somewhat differently than to other deaths (12). Still, and given the fact that she has, by admission, set out on a "narrow course," Kubler-Ross has given us what have to be seen as the best treatments provided yet of many problems of the dying. She has popularized the subject with commendable success and in a poetic writing style which makes her works easily and comfortably read. Kubler-Ross has made contributions of immeasurable importance to care of the terminally ill and to the dignity of dying. In the early part of *On Death and Dying* (13) she protests our social use of euphemisms, our denial of a child's right to visit his dying parent, our efforts to make the dead seem only to be sleeping, our hiding of truth from those who should not be deceived.

Jeanne Quint, a nurse-sociologist, has added a dimension which extends beyond the family.

> The majority of nurses . . . do not enjoy assignments to dying patients . . . . Many nurses describe themselves as ill at ease in conversing with a dying patient, particularly if he wants to talk about his death or related matters. This problem is intensified, however, when nurses are told that the patient is not to be informed of his diagnosis or prognosis. (14–18)

Some of the typical and unnecessary problems associated with dying in an institution are being alleviated by developers of *hospices* in various European, American, and Canadian communities. A hospice in New Haven, Connecticut, patterned on St. Christopher's in London, is intended as "a therapeutic environment designed from the patient's point of view," and is for persons with terminal illness and also their families if desired, including children and pets. More a complex of ideas than simply a place, and neither a hospital nor a nursing home, a hospice emphasizes a dignified and humane combination of a home-like atmosphere with the actual home. Also included are various kinds of postbereavement help for survivors, ranging from peer support activities to direct assistance from social workers as well as from professionally qualified counselors who are occasionally available to help bereaved persons. Plans for this kind of hospice centers are being implemented in Montreal, New York City, and Harrisburg, in more than 25 other communities such as Kansas City (19, 20), and in perhaps as many as 150 others at this writing.

Kubler-Ross suggests it might help if we could speak of dying as "an intrinsic part of life" (21), as we speak freely of childbirth, and she adds (22) that the question should not be on the order of, "Do I tell?" but rather, "How do I share this information?" Kubler-Ross points out that the more people in the patient's environment who are aware of the diagnosis of a malignancy, the sooner the patient himself will realize the true state of affairs anyway (23).

Glaser and Strauss (24) have described four stages of moribund patients' awareness of impending death: a) closed awareness, in which the person has no idea of the truth of his condition; b) suspicious awareness, where there is premonition of dying; c) mutual pretense, an anxiety-producing stage in which the person knows he is dying but pretends not to know; and d) open awareness, in which the person both knows he is dying and is ready and willing to talk about it. But Kubler-Ross is of the opinion that instead of talking, the more common tendency is to keep smiling and pretend that one is happy, even when everyone in the situation knows what is happening, but each is fearful of sharing with the other (25).

Beyond this, we have the following sensible observation from Quint:

> Since dying is a social experience as well as a biological one, it behooves us to consider seriously the consequences for patients who are not informed. These patients cannot talk to their relatives about it, nor can they act toward themselves as if they were dying. They cannot say good-byes or openly plan for the future of their families, nor can the hospital staff share this final social experience with these patients. (26)

Kubler-Ross suggests that if family members can be helped to grow together toward acceptance of the inevitable, much unnecessary suffering can be avoided (27). She says that virtually all terminally ill persons know about their impending deaths anyway (28), whether they are told explicitly or not. Her reports state that several terminally ill patients she has known have asked to meet with their families in the psychiatrist's presence in order to "drop the facade" and to enjoy the last few weeks together fully (29). "Things happen," Mervyn adds (30), "as [the patient] senses that his care is becoming different." Movement from home to hospital to nursing home is likely to provide clues as to the status of health (31).

"Often his location on the nursing unit changes as his condition deteriorates—from a four-bed room to a single room, or closer or further away from the nursing office. . . . Staff members may avoid him. Answers to his questions may be so evasive that he feels puzzled, helpless, and hopeless" (32).

Another nurse has reported her experiences with a patient who, as is true of so many, had not been "told":

> A woman, whose husband had decided she was not to know her diagnosis or her prognosis, made this observation to the hospital chaplain. "I know what I have, that I have cancer, and that I am going to die." The chaplain continued to see her on a regular basis, and she talked openly with him about her death, but she continued to pretend with her husband and the staff until the end. (33)

Kubler-Ross says that family members go through stages of adjustment similar to that which patients experience; there may be disbelief, denial, shopping around from physician to physician, trips to faith healers and famed clinics (34). Then, and very much "depending on the patient's attitude, awareness, and ability to communicate," the family

> . . . undergoes certain changes. If they are able to share their common concerns, they can take care of important matters and under less pressure of time and emotions. If each one tries to keep a secret from the other, they will keep an artificial barrier between them which will make it difficult for any preparatory grief for the patient or his

> family.   The end result will be more dramatic than for
> those who can talk and cry together at times. (35)

This "preparatory grief" is important to the bereavement
process, Kubler-Ross and many others believe (36, 37).
"The more this grief can be expressed before death, the less
unbearable it becomes afterward" (38); however, while
preparatory grieving helps, it does not *resolve* postbereavement grieving.   Still, expressions of such preparatory grief
and sharing one's sorrow with the dying person (who also
wishes to share sorrow) is far superior to "a make-believe
mask which the patient can see through anyway" (39).
Genuine emotion is much easier to take.

The British psychiatrist C. M. Parkes, whose research interests have centered less on dying than on bereaved surviving, agrees that the sharing of preparatory grief can be facilitative (40), particularly when spouses can share future
planning of the apparent survivor and when the dying partner can take comfort from knowing that those who live on
will be cared for.   Parkes believes that this kind of fore-
knowledge is far better than the postbereavement situation
which is likely to face the survivor who has been emotionally unprepared for a predictable death (41).   Parkes adds
that despite the acute hurt of anticipatory grief, it can lead
eventually to a kind of serenity for the persons who share
it—and that postbereavement memories of the dying time
will be more satisfying than will be the memories held by
others who have not shared the sad truth with close ones
during their dying (42).

And finally, attention is invited to the comment offered
by psychiatrist Richard Vanden Bergh (1966):

> There are reports in the literature about patients who, told
> of their impending death, have used all their remaining time
> in a most constructive manner. Equally numerous are re-
> ports of patients who have become extremely depressed,
> spending their remaining time in abject misery. I believe
> that each patient must be assessed individually, and then

> told or not told according to the specific reaction predicted. Even then, many mistakes will be made. Perhaps the only rule one can make, with any degree of certainty, is that if the physician decides to tell the patient the truth, he must be prepared to stand by the patient and help him work through any untoward reaction that might result. (43)

The observation must be made that in the review of research and opinion which was basic to this book not one case was found in which any competent observer reported anything like permanent "extreme depression" resulting from receipt of a terminal diagnosis, or of any persons who spent "their remaining time in abject misery." It is probable that many persons do die in depression and misery, and it may be a matter of record or of research evidence that some such persons would have died more happily had they not been told they were dying, but such evidence has escaped the present investigator and did not emerge in studies on which this book is based. It seems likely that cases of prolonged extreme depression and abject misery arise from faulty psychological management of the total situation, and that depressions extending to death indicate that the person was not permitted to work his way past the transient depression which, obviously, must be a part of any situation which all know will terminate in death.

However, even if there are known cases of stable and unyielding adverse responses to a fatal prognosis *which would not have been present anyway*, to leave the "tell-or-don't-tell" decision to the physician is one of those absurdities that seems dictated more by primitive tradition and institutional routine than by reason. In hospitals, the patient's total care is the responsibility of the physician in charge of the case, but why this should extend to granting that person sole responsibility for determining whether or not the patient should be told of his imminent death is not altogether sensible. Physicians are not, usually, psychologists, and usually are without significant preparation in mental health endeavors. Of various professionals who are available to make such decisions, the physician may in fact be the least prepared to make one in which the patient's emotional well-being is at stake. Aside from the psychiatrists who are often available, many hospitals employ nurses and others with substantial training and graduate degrees in counseling, appropriate psychology specialties, or in psychiatric care; many chaplains are especially prepared in therapeutic counseling (44–48). It is not unusual for social workers to be skilled in assessment of personality dynamics and in communication skills. Circumstances become flatly bizarre when sensitive and intelligent nurses (as one example), under orders not to tell the family that someone important to them is dying, have had to keep a dead patient locked away from his visiting relatives until the physician could be located at a party and summoned to the hospital to advise the family that the patient died some little time ago.

Perhaps the best guidance on the matter of whether or not to tell has been provided by Verwoerdt, who offered several key questions for determining the readiness of a patient to know the truth about his condition (49). First, what is the status of the person's emotional and intellectual resources? In short, what is the patient's level of maturity? Associated with this question are allied questions relating to his past successes in handling stress, the presence or absence of emotional difficulties beyond those which are normal, the presence or absence of psychosomatic distress, the intellectual capacity of the person to understand what is happening to him, and so on. Second, one needs to be aware of how much the dying person already knows. Factors associated with this question include the number and nature of previous contacts with physicians, the type of medical facility in which the patient is being treated, the amount of discomfort he is experiencing, and the family's medical history. Third, what personal meaning may the disease have to the patient? This question is a particularly important one if the same disease caused the death of some family member or close friend and if, accordingly, the disease carries emotional loading for the present patient. The last of Verwoerdt's questions relates to how much the patient seems to want to know, a question which relies for its answer on substantial skill in assessment of verbal and non-verbal communications from the central person. The patient may exhibit a preference to deny, and at least one physician has argued that the right of denial is the patient's, and that he should be permitted that right until he is prepared to hear more of the truth of the situation (50).

The same rules apply when a child is dying. The question of telling is answered in large measure by assessing how much the child seems to want to know and how much he surmises from his own physical situation and discomfort. "Depending on their age and the illness, most children benefit from explanations about what is being done to them and why. They are relieved by being told directly that they will be given medicine for pain and will not be left alone for long" (51). When possible, the ideal is to keep the child from having to contend with the psychological pain of fear and mystery along with the physical pain which is a part of the disease process. "When a child obtains the right to speak and to share the knowledge of others concerning his body, he acquires an intellectual control over his fears and an objectivity regarding his distressing fantasies" (52). Even young children pick up internal and external clues about their condition and experience isolation and withdrawal as death nears (53). However, unlike the adult, the child may develop resentment when he discovers his parents are not omnipotent in relieving his discomfort and getting him home (54). Fortunately, youngsters under 15 account for only about 5 per cent of the annual United States death rate (55). (The death rate of children in 1900 was about half of the total.)

HELPING THE DYING

Counselors, psychologists, and psychiatrists are not always available to offer direct help to dying people. This will be the job of nurses, attending physicians, members of the immediate family, appropriate clergy, and others whose job definitions and social roles put them in direct contact with people who are dying. Outside helpers may in fact be helpful in a variety of ways, but their principal usefulness will be with the family and with close friends who happen to be in the death environment. It is not usual for such people to have many direct contacts with the moribund individual unless they themselves are among his family or closest friends (or, in Jewish tradition, among those who share responsibility for being always at the bedside of the dying person, who is never abandoned during this time). It follows that professional helpers and concerned friends will probably best help the dying by, first, understanding what is going on with dying people, and second, helping grieving persons in the prebereavement stage to help most effectively their loved ones who are in the final days or weeks of life.

Living While Dying

"Perhaps we need to remind ourselves," Quint suggested, "that patients who are dying are not just dying. They are also living. Whether or not they have the opportunity to live their final human experiences to the fullest—each in his own way—is influenced in great measure by us who take care of them" (56). And Kubler-Ross tells us that dying patients seem to have a need to care for themselves and to keep their dignity and independence as long as possible (57). Accordingly, we can best help the dying by helping them to live rather than simply to "vegetate" in some "inhuman manner" (58) or to occupy themselves learning how to be "acceptable dying patients" (59). Nurse-clinician Gyulay agrees that too often we are too quick to do *to*, *through*, and *around* those who are dying (60).

Much is made by many knowledgeable observers of the desirability of dying at home; however, the sword has two edges. A lengthy terminal illness at home may become a very real burden which strains or exhausts the physical, emotional, and financial resources of the family. There will be times when an influential outsider may have to put pressure on the family to admit its dying member to a nursing home in the best interests of everyone's emotional and physical health. When this measure is required, it must be kept in mind that the family will probably experience guilt in removing its dying member to outside care, and attention to such feelings is essential. The guilt and related discomfort will probably be less in evidence if the dying person is comatose, incoherent, or senile than if he is alert, aware, and verbal (61). It must be borne in mind that one of the family's most difficult adjustment problems is that of turning over responsibilities for total care of their loved person to strangers, who expect them to stand by and keep out of the way. It is a particularly difficult problem when children are involved (62–64).

Talking it Over

According to Parkes most patients with terminal illnesses know what is coming, and most welcome an opportunity to talk about it (65). They are particularly receptive to empathic listeners who do not insist on "jollying them along." The point is reinforced by Kubler-Ross (66), who says, "Dying persons will welcome someone who is willing to talk with them about their dying but will allow them to keep their defenses as long as they need them."

As living people often cannot live comfortably until they rid themselves of some of the guilt they carry around, so too, some dying people cannot die comfortably until they are rid of their guilt. Kubler-Ross says, "We are always amazed how one session can relieve a patient of a tremendous burden and wonder why it is so difficult for staff and family to elicit their needs, since it often requires nothing more but an open question" (67). She insists that the dying patients who do best in their dying are those "who have been encouraged to express their rage, to cry in preparatory grief, and to express their fears and fantasies to someone who can sit quietly and listen" (68). Kubler-Ross cautions that while dying people may want very much to talk about their dying and will respond with relief when others are prepared to spend time with them for that purpose, the need to talk about this subject is not obsessional. The patient who wishes to talk about his death on one day may, on the next, wish to talk "only about the pleasant aspects of life," and she recommends that we respect the person's wishes in this regard (69).

> *Light cares speak,*
> *when mighty griefs are dumb.*
> *SAMUEL DANIEL*
> *COMPLAINT OF ROSAMOND*

Parkes also has been impressed by the patient's need to talk (70). He is particularly impressed by the strategic circumstances of nurses, who he believes can be particularly helpful and who, Vanden Bergh believed, are terribly important to dying people (71).

> Dying patients, in talking to me about their nurses, stress how important it is for them to feel that the nurses are constantly nearby. They do not expect the nurse to come in and talk with them at length, but when the nurse merely looks in on them from time to time, asks how they are, and sees if they need anything, their general sense of well-being and security is increased. I believe this is a universal need of dying patients. (72)

Parkes (73) argues that nurses must be free to sit and talk with patients who are dying, and without feeling guilty as Mervyn believes many nurses do (74), and without being reprimanded by superiors and told to get back to work—various observers have suggested that for nurses to talk with patients *is* work. Kubler-Ross would probably agree; she found that "When a dying person asks someone to talk with him now, tomorrow may be too late" (75).

We must not become so intense in our concern with what professional therapists and close friends can offer in a death situation that we forget most immediate responsibilities lie with the family, and the family should be encouraged and permitted to take care of their own while they are dying. Fulton and Fulton say that dying is an extraordinarily complicated affair (76), full of emotional, educational, familial, property, personal, economic, and social implications which really must be worked out by the kinship and friendship groups involved, ideally with full participation of the dying member.

It is anyone's guess who a dying person will choose to talk with and to share terribly intimate and important aspects of his living and his dying; this may not have much to do with long-term or depth relationships between the two but is often a response to needs of the moment. One who is not selected by the dying person for such an encounter should not be offended, since no offense has been intended.

THE KUBLER-ROSS
PSYCHOLOGICAL PHASES OF DYING

According to Kubler-Ross dying people—other than those whose deaths are sudden and unforeseen—go through five distinct phases in dying, not necessarily in sequence but each different from the other. Counselors and others who would be helpful in times of bereavement—unless they are clergymen or nurses, too—usually will not have much direct contact with dying persons in the normal course of events. However, it is useful for helpers to be familiar with the psychological phenomena of dying so that they can assist surviving members of the family and the family's friends to understand what is happening during the dying process. Kubler-Ross' stages are 1) denial, 2) anger, 3) bargaining, 4) depression, and 5) acceptance. The following discussions elucidate each of the stages of the "Kubler-Ross Syndrome" as she and others have defined them.

Denial

Denial is a widely used psychological defense. It is a process of refusing, at least temporarily, to acknowledge or believe that some factual event is really true. In bereavement, denial "functions as a buffer after unexpected shocking news, allows the patient to collect himself and, with time, mobilize other, less radical defenses" (77). It seems to operate particularly strongly with mothers facing the impending death of a child.(78), and it has been observed that the death of a grown child is a particularly traumatic experience for surviving parents, one of the most difficult of grief reactions, and one which is perhaps hospitable to a denial defense. The problem with denial, psychologically, is that it cannot operate on an unconscious level to repress unwanted ideas or events—denial activity has to be maintained consciously, at considerable psychological cost (79). That makes denial a very tiring defense.

The individual's first reaction to news that he is dying is likely to be numb shock, momentary speechlessness, a blank look. Some of the physiological signs of shock may be present. These include the vacant look with dilated pupils, shallow and irregular breathing, fast but weak pulse, cool and clammy skin with perspiration, and sometimes nausea. The individual may be unusually restless or without discernible alertness, and marked thirst is common. Breathing may be faster than usual, and anxious deep breathing or sighing may be manifested. These symptoms are not likely to last for any appreciable length of time unless the individual faints—which he may do—and the initial sense of shock and feeling of numbness will disappear, at least for awhile. It may reappear occasionally, as the individual is brought back time and again to a recognition of what has happened, before he really assimilates it.

Shock is a physiological defense, and once the initial shock has gone, denial appears as the first of the psychological defenses. The individual whose death sentence has been pronounced may say, "No, it can't be me," or "No, not me," or "It can't be true," or simply "No, no, no."

Denial: Say it isn't true and it won't be. Everyone will think it, virtually everyone will say it. Anxious denial following a fatal diagnostic presentation is more common when the confrontation has been handled prematurely or too abruptly (80), but the extent to which denial will be used by the dying person seems to have quite a lot to do with that individual's makeup.

Persons will use the same defenses in a death situation that they use regularly in coping with stress. Kubler-Ross suggests that people who routinely use denial as a main defense in their lives will use it much more extensively when confronted with a death message than will others (81). Those who routinely follow a stratagem of facing stress and dealing with it openly will do so when they learn they are about to die. So the extent to which denial is employed depends largely on who the person is and how he is integrated emotionally. It is interesting to note in passing the Kubler-Ross observation that physicians who need denial themselves will find it in their patients, and that those physicians who can talk easily about terminal illness will find their patients better able to face and to acknowledge it (82). Still, despite their own personality structures and the inhibitions or openness of their physicians, Kubler-Ross insists that "Denial, at least partial denial, is used by almost all patients, not only during the first stages of illness or following confrontation, but also later on from time to time" (83).

The denial defense is likely to be strongest "at the very beginning of a serious illness more so than towards the end of life" (84), but *it will recur later* and should be expected, without the senseless exercise of pointing out to a dying person who seems to have accepted his own demise that now he is suddenly using denial. There is no need to play psychotherapeutic games with dying people who come up with occasional inconsistencies; the inconsistencies should simply be accepted by the helper. Dying people will exhibit denial—strongly at first, but later, too.

It was mentioned earlier that one of the most helpful things people at a deathbed can do is to be available to let the dying person talk, to ventilate his feelings. But Kubler-Ross says that during such interviews (always at the patient's convenience and only when he is able to face things) the person with whom he is talking should be alert to signs of denial and, if they appear, "gently terminate the interview" (85).

Another aspect of denial is making the assumption that one's physician doesn't know what he is doing. The dying patient, frequently supported by family and friends, then begins shopping around for other medical people in hopes of finding one who offers a less morbid diagnosis or who can offer a "new" treatment or even a tried and true "old" one that will work. People will often travel long distances in this kind of search and perhaps pursue various new quackeries or engage in many negative consultations with ethical practitioners before they can find someone who will pronounce them fit. They are likely to stay with that physician until they die.

Medical quackery is still around. The charlatan can easily be spotted because he tends to use special or secret machines; guarantees a quick and/or easy cure; advertises, often with testimonials; demands recognition from competent medical professionals but refuses to allow his technique to be subjected to the rigors of controlled testing; asserts that he is being persecuted by organized ethical medical practitioners; and makes a great point of his method's being superior to surgery, drugs, and similar accepted treatments. The quack frequently uses the mails for purposes of consultation (as do some "psychotherapists" who are unqualified as psychologists or counselors). While his victims are commonly the ignorant or foolish, many people who should know better consult the quack as a last resort, but the net effect is generally a passing of cash from their hands into those of the charlatan and perhaps a loss of some of the time they have remaining.

One of the current examples of quasimedical quackery which feeds into a denial system can be found in modern entrepeneurs who propose to deep-freeze the moribund, promising that at some later time when a cure for their terminal illness has been found they can be thawed and brought back for appropriate treatment to continue their interrupted lives. The idea may sound good enough on first presentation, but a little thought makes it substantially less appealing, one of the primary objections being that one would have to flash-freeze the dying individual before his actual death. The ethical, religious, and legal issues involved in that kind of transaction are enough to boggle the mind.

As mentioned before, a defense commonly used by relatives is one in which the gravity of a loved person's condition is played down; the same thing happens with patients who are dying and who are employing denial. According to Kubler-Ross, listening to a patient who is using denial "may seem like listening to a patient with a minor ailment, nothing as serious as a life-threatening condition" (86). This seems to be particularly true of the patient who discusses his situation very openly with some person, yet feels compelled to protect others by pretending with them to be getting better (87).

The denial defense is usually only temporary, although it recurs from time to time; normally it is transitory and is replaced by partial acceptance of the truth. Few persons continue to use denial, although elements of the defense, according to Kubler-Ross, will persist to the end, and the defense can even be used for positive effect (88).

> It is more meaningful for the patient and his family to see that the illness does not totally disrupt a household or completely deprive all members of any pleasurable activities; rather, the illness may allow for a gradual adjustment and change toward the kind of home it is going to be when the patient is no longer around. Just as the terminally ill patient cannot face death all the time, a family member cannot and should not exclude all other interactions for the sake of being with the patient exclusively. He too has a

need to deny or avoid the sad realities at times in order to
face them better when his presence is really needed (89).

It may be that *hope* is a kind of denial, and one of the
most common strategies of hospital staff in dealing with
dying persons and their families is to reinforce hope by re-
ferring to ongoing research, the possibility of remission, and
the like. (According to Mauksch (90), hospital personnel
reinforce denial in dying patients.) Kubler-Ross says "It is
not in human nature to accept the finality of death without
leaving a door open for some hope" (91), and it probably
does no harm since, for the dying person, there is little else
available.

> *Because I could not stop for Death,*
> *He kindly stopped for me;*
> *The carriage held but just ourselves*
> *And Immortality.*
>
> *EMILY DICKINSON*
> *BECAUSE I COULD NOT*
> *STOP FOR DEATH*

Kubler-Ross reports that the one thing that usually persists through all the stages of dying is hope. The patients
whom she studied expressed the greatest confidence in physicians who allowed for hope—realistic or not—and appreciated it when hope was offered in spite of bad news. Kubler-
Ross says this does not mean that physicians have to tell
lies, it means merely "that we share with them the hope
that something unforeseen may happen, that they may have
a remission, that they will live longer than is expected. If a
patient stops expressing hope, it is usually a sign of imminent death" (92).

Gyulay, a nurse-clinician who for years has specialized in
care of children with terminal cancer, discusses hope as
follows:

> With relapse or metastases, the reality of the truth of the situation is brought home. The first relapse is the worst and the most difficult of all, although each change brings with it the deepest heartache that a family can cope with. As each spread or relapse takes place, hope undergoes a change. From hope at the beginning that the diagnosis is not serious, it changes to the hope for cure or long remission, then to the hope that their loved one will die in dignity without pain, and that after death the family will be able to go through the grief process without "losing their minds." (93)

Yet, Kubler-Ross points up two difficulties with hope which can get in the way. She says the first problem with hope comes when the patient is in need of hope yet the medical staff conveys hopelessness, which presents a particularly painful state of affairs for the patient. The second fault with hope arises with the family's refusal to accept what is really happening—the family's refusal to abandon hope when the patient is ready to go and experiences frustration on top of the difficulties of dying because his closest persons cannot accept his death with him (94). The occasional insistence by some families that life-support equipment be used to maintain heart and lung activity long after a person has experienced brain death and is clinically deceased is an example of denial exhibited by survivors (95). Further, hope for survival occasionally persists among close persons beyond death; this is regarded as a symptom of pathological grief (96).

Anger

The second psychological phase of dying described by Kubler-Ross is that of anger, the "Why me?" stage. This angry stage includes envy of living and healthy persons and annoyance with those who do not have to face death so soon (97). The person may be angry with himself for being "weak" or even for committing the social error of letting his physicians and nurses down (98).

The angry patient will raise his voice, he will make demands, he will complain and ask to be given attention, perhaps as the last loud cry of "I am alive, don't forget that. You can hear my voice, I am not dead yet!" The patient who is respected and understood, who is given attention and a little time, will soon lower his voice and reduce his angry demands. (99)

Kubler-Ross adds that the stage of anger is a difficult one to cope with from the point of view of family and staff since anger is displaced in all directions, at times almost at random. She calls it the patient's "pig stage." He believes that his physicians are no good, to be sure, but nurses are more handy and so are more often a target of anger. The anger may be seen by hospital staff personnel as violating the self-image they have of themselves as helpers. Patients who exhibit normal anger may be resented by physicians and nurses as enacting indecently hostile behaviors which are inadequately respectful of them and which, indeed, attack the hospital staff's culture and rules (100, 101). Mervyn commented that "dying patients who manage to remain agreeable and pleasant have a much better chance of geting attention than do those who fight death and become angry" (102).

Kubler-Ross says it's a tragedy when we take the patient's anger personally and don't take into account the reasons for that anger. It has little or nothing to do with the people who are targets of the anger.

As the staff or family reacts personally to this anger, they respond with increasing anger on their part, only feeding into the patient's hostile behavior. They may use avoidance and shorten the visits or the rounds, or they may get into unnecessary arguments by defending their stand, not knowing that the issue is often totally irrelevant. (103)

The most difficult dying patient, according to Kubler-Ross, is the "rich and controlling VIP, as he is to lose the very things that made life so comfortable for him." In the end, we are all the same, but the VIPs "cannot admit that. . . . They fight it to the end . . . they provoke rejection and anger, and are yet the most desperate of them all" (104).

> *I am prepared to meet my Maker.*
> *Whether my Maker is prepared*
> *for the great ordeal of meeting*
> *me is another matter.*
>
> *WINSTON CHURCHILL*
> *COMMENT ON 75TH BIRTHDAY*

Bargaining

Bargaining is the third stage, and Kubler-Ross describes the patient's bargaining this way: "If God has decided to take me from this earth and he did not respond to my angry pleas, he may be more favorable if I ask nicely" (105). The phase is typical during periods of remission in a disease process, according to Gyulay (106), and is akin, Kubler-Ross believes, to the strategy of young children who first may make angry demands and then, if those demands are not met, put the demands in the form of a favor—usually in return for some behavior on their part of which the parent will approve.

Bargaining is an effort to postpone; Kubler-Ross says it includes elements of a prize offered to the dying person in return for his good behavior, and typically includes some kind of deadline imposed by the patient himself. Bargaining includes an implicit promise that if one death postponement is granted, the patient will not ask for anything more—but of course he does, like a child.

It is typical for patients to try to bargain for a little more time—an extension of life—or a few days without pain or discomfort in return for his promise to dedicate the remainder of his life to God, or to attend church regularly, or to stop beating his wife, or to leave his body to science (107).

24

Those are the elements: good behaviors promised in return for the favor.

> *Here I lie, Martin Elginbrodde;*
> *Have mercy on my soul, Lord God—*
> *As I would do was I Lord God*
> *And ye was Martin Elginbrodde.*
>
> *(WIDELY REPORTED*
> *BUT NEVER SEEN)*
> *EPITAPH*

Kubler-Ross tells us that the expression of a wish during bargaining may tip off a guilt problem the patient is having (108). If so, the patient should be given opportunity to work out his guilt, particularly if the guilt and his attendant fears are irrational. (When elements of strong guilt or irrationality appear, the helper who is not a mental health professional would do well to suggest calling in a psychologist or a qualified counselor.) The Catholic Church has known for centuries about the desirability of talking away one's guilt, and whether their historical reasons have been theological or psychological, their priests have doubtlessly done immense good for hundreds of thousands of dying people who have been given opportunity for that last confession.

Depression

The fourth phase of psychological response to grief is one of depression, and Kubler-Ross has been careful to distinguish between the two kinds of depression which dying persons will experience at different times, and which must be responded to in different ways (109). The two types of depression are *reactive* depression and *prepatory* depression.

The distinction is not new; it was made at least as early as 1586, when it was recognized that some depressions result from physiological stimuli whereas others relate to environmental stimuli. Today, the two classes of depression would be called *endogenous* (from within the body) or *exogenous* (from without), because emotional phenomena can be related to either or both, so that a kind of *reactive* or *exogenous* depression could result from receipt of bad news, from financial reverses and the like, whereas physical breakdown could result in an *endogenous* depression (110), or what Kubler-Ross has called a *preparatory depression*. Whether the depression is endogenous or exogenous doesn't need to concern us here, since the signs and behaviors will be essentially similar, and since we will be looking more closely at depressions a little later, when we consider post-bereavement reactions of survivors.

Reactive Depression. The terms *reactive depression* and *depressive neurosis* are synonymous. Either way, the term applies to an acute and intensely lonely emotional response to a particularly distressing environmental event which includes relatively low morale and self-deprecation. Problems of sleep and appetite may be reported, with resultant fatigue, lowered initiative and activity, difficulties of concentration, and somatic distresses of various kinds. Facial features are typically dull. Feelings of guilt and borderline anger or hostility are common, and the person is likely to experience himself as being inadequate, discouraged, apprehensive, tense, and without self-confidence, and to exhibit more dependency than is usual for him. Occasionally, emotional withdrawal with unusual introversion may be seen.

When a reactive depression occurs in a dying person, as Kubler-Ross says it will, the usual therapeutic technique of working with the client over a period of weeks or perhaps months to alleviate distress and reduce depression by means that will provide for long-term satisfactory adjustment just isn't appropriate. Instead, a short-cut approach is recommended; it can provide temporary relief at best, but that is sufficient under the circumstances. Kubler-Ross says that a reactive depression in the dying patient can be aided by such simple measures as reassurance, building self-esteem, making sure the dying woman (as one example) knows her household and children are being managed in her absence, and so on (111). While on the surface it may seem brutal to ask a dying mother to train her successor, there are two principal benefits in doing precisely that when circumstances do not argue forcibly against the procedure. First, in seeking her instructions, adult family members reassure the dying mother that her children will be continuing to receive the level of care she provided; and second, the sanctioning of certain behaviors by the dying mother seems to make those arrangements more acceptable to the children, who will regard the surrogate's activities as having their mother's approval (112).

Obviously, the idea should not be conveyed that things are just as good as when the ill person was active and around, but the dying individual can achieve some level of comfort from realizing that things have not been allowed to completely go to hell in his or her absence. [It can be helpful in a time of reactive depression to be bluntly encouraging and cheerful, and certainly to be available and present whenever possible.] In reactive depression the patient has a lot to share and requires much verbal interaction and intervention. Weisman and Hackett have urged that dying persons be treated with the same respect which would be shown any members of the family and encouraged to contribute opinions on family problems and plans (113).

Preparatory Depression. Kubler-Ross describes the second type of depression. Preparatory depression

> is necessary and beneficial if the patient is to die in a stage of acceptance and peace. Only patients who have been able to work through their anguish and anxieties are able to achieve this stage. If this reassurance could be shared with their families, they too could be spared much unnecessary anguish. (114)

The sort of emotional propping-up which is appropriate in a time of *reactive* depression is not a good tactic in *preparatory* depression.

. . . the patient should not be encouraged to look at the sunny side of things, as this would mean he should not contemplate his impending death. It'd be contraindicated to tell him not to be sad, since all of us are tremendously sad when we lose our beloved person. The patient is in the process of losing everything and everybody he loves. If he is allowed to express his sorrow he will find a final acceptance much easier, and he will be grateful to find those who can sit with him during this stage of depression without constantly telling him not to be sad. (115)

> *I am bored with it all.*
> *WINSTON CHURCHILL*
> *(ON HIS DEATHBED)*

Preparatory depression is usually silent. "There is little or no need for words. It is much more a feeling that can be mutually expressed and is often done better with a touch of a hand, a stroking of the hair, or just a silent sitting together" (116). "It's a time," Kubler-Ross says, "When too much interference from visitors who try to cheer [the patient] up hinders his emotional preparation rather than enhances it" (117). In both reactive and preparatory depression one can expect to find the dying person spending a lot of time sleeping; and in either case it is not a sleep of rest—it is a sleep of avoidance (118).

Acceptance

According to Kubler-Ross the final psychological phase through which dying people go is one she calls "acceptance," an attitudinal set which is apparently not to be confused with simple resignation (119). Osis and Haraldsson have, in a somewhat different context, described a time of elation, serenity, and peace (120), developing in some 90% of patients in which it is observed within an hour before death.

If a patient has had time and has been given some help in working through the . . . stages, he will reach a stage during which he is neither depressed nor angry about his fate . . . [He'll be able to] contemplate his coming end with a certain degree of quiet expectation. He will be tired, and in most cases quite weak. He will also have a need to doze off to sleep often and in brief intervals, which is different from the need to sleep during the time of depression. This is not a sleep of avoidance or a period of rest to get relief from pain, discomfort, or itching. It is a gradually increasing need to extend the hours of sleep very similar to that of a newborn child but in reverse order. (121)

> *Let us cross the river*
> *and rest in the shade.*
> *STONEWALL JACKSON*
> *(ON HIS DEATHBED)*

This is the time when the patient has come to accept that nothing more can be done for him. During this time of acceptance the patient seems to take comfort in knowing that he is not forgotten and that people will want to take time to be with him (122), and he senses that his loved ones have not worked through their anticipatory grief so well that they have already given up on him—the dying patient should not be compelled to grieve the perceived loss of his family's love, as well (123).

Not long ago I sat at the bedside of an 84-year-old dying patient. She was very close to death. A staff member came into the room and cheerily said, "Well, Mrs. J., how are we today?" (I noticed questions directed to elderly dying patients are often phrased with a "we" as if the patient lacked the dignity of a separate identity as "you" and also perhaps because using "we" implies concern about one's own feelings as well as the patient's.) Mrs. J. moved herself up in bed with her elbows and said in her most regal British accent: "Well, my child, I don't know how *we* are feeling, but *I* am doing something I shall not do again.   I am dying." (124)

> *It's been very interesting.*
> *MARY WORTLEY MONTAGU*
> *(ON HER DEATHBED)*

Kubler-Ross cautions that the acceptance stage should not be confused with a happy time. She says it is almost devoid of feeling.

> It is as if the pain had gone, the struggle is over and there comes a time for "the final rest before the long journey" . . . .   This is also the time during which the family usually needs more help, understanding, and support than the patient himself. While the dying patient has found some peace and acceptance, his circle of interest diminishes. He wishes to be left alone or at least not stirred up by news and problems of the outside world. Visitors are often not desired and if they come, the patient is no longer in a talkative mood. He often requests limitations on the number of people and prefers short visits. . . . He may just hold our hand and ask us to sit in silence. (125)

As Kubler-Ross suggests, the helper should not insist on conversation, nor should the family—all should let the dying person know it is okay to say nothing. There may be times during the acceptance phase when the dying person will prefer not to see the helper at all. As Samuel Johnson put it, "Every man must walk down to the grave alone."

> *I pray you see me safe up,*
> *and for my coming down*
> *let me shift for myself.*
> *SIR THOMAS MORE*
> *(ON HIS WAY TO THE SCAFFOLD)*

No argument is offered here that the patient should be abandoned as his life nears its end. Gyulay says that too often, "Communication frequently becomes a problem during the terminal phase; rounds become shorter, visits with the patient decrease, lights are answered less promptly, less talking and listening with the patient and his family leave them abandoned at the most crucial time of their defenselessness" (126).

She cautions that "No matter how comatose a patient is, there needs to be awareness of what is said around his bed." She encourages talking to the patient "even when he is not alert, for the possibility is that his level of awareness is greater than it appears to be." Talking and touching are important, Gyulay believes, for patient, staff and family (127).

It is a question of reasonable balance. Kubler-Ross tells us that if they are understood and not intruded upon unnecessarily, many patients will come to acceptance pretty much by themselves (128). Still, "There are a few patients who fight to the end, who struggle to keep a hope that makes it almost impossible to reach this stage of acceptance." She further comments, "The family and staff may consider these patients tough and strong, they may encourage the fight for life to the end, and they may implicitly communicate that accepting one's end is regarded as a cowardly giving up, as a deceit or, worse yet, a rejection of the family" (129).

One should try to bear in mind, whether one is a helper or a griever, that there is no need for toughness and strongness at the end. A person in the terminal stage of dying has his peace and he has his dignity, and if that person is accepting it, others should try to accept it, too.

First our pleasures die—and then
Our hopes, and then our fears—and when

These are dead, the debt is due,
Dust claims dust—and we die too.

SHELLEY
DEATH

Kubler-Ross suggests that at the end, "When we have worked and given, enjoyed ourselves and suffered, we are going back to the stage that we started out with and the circle of life is closed" (130). During the acceptance phase, the patient will exhibit needs to detach himself—but this doesn't mean that anyone is being rejected. It is difficult for families to understand and accept this behavior when in his final phase the patient may ask to be visited by only a few more friends, then by his children, and finally perhaps only by his wife. This is how the person manages his final separation (131). It is the most heartbreaking time for the family. "They do not understand that a dying man who has found peace and acceptance in his death will have to separate himself, step by step, from his environment, including his most loved ones. How could he ever be ready to die if he continued to hold onto the meaningful relationships of which a man has so many?" (132)

The dying person does not have to fight, his fight is over—and he is not just giving up, since events are far beyond his control. He certainly is not rejecting the family; all he is doing is preparing to make his last trip alone. And as for the final moments, Gyulay's advice to other nurses concerning child deaths can easily be applied also to adults and the thoughts about parents expanded to include spouses and friends.

> When death is imminent, parents should be told and provided privacy and support in the manner that they want and with whom they want; this includes siblings. If they want to hold their child, it should be allowed. It should be explained to them that if the child dies while in their arms . . . they have not caused the death. This has to be said in so many words. This is no time to be coy or to

mince words; the actual word "death" must be used. Expressions such as "very critical," "it's near," "it looks very bad" are oftentimes used by the staff to escape the painful reality that the child is indeed dying. . . . Tissues should be close at hand, saying nonverbally that tears are appropriate, and the staff not only understands but shares that box! (133)

Now cracks a noble heart.
Goodnight, sweet prince,
And flights of angels
Sing thee to thy rest!
        SHAKESPEARE
        HAMLET

DEATH: THE OSIS-HARALDSSON
AND MOODY INVESTIGATIONS

Death has been defined as the condition which exists when there is absence in some individual of clinically detectable vital signs; or when there is absence of brain wave activity as measured by an electroencephalograph machine; or when there is an irreversible loss of vital functions (134). What ultimately becomes of dead people, of their souls (or whatever), has stimulated interesting speculation for as long as humans have had the capacity to wonder.

While in large measure the questions associated with "life after death" are the province of theologians, philosophers, poets, and perhaps of mystics, some fairly recent research has provided insights into what may be experienced by at least some persons during near death, and possibly even during death itself. Although this work is highly tentative at the present writing, it deserves reporting here because it is far less speculative than previous hypotheses, based as it is on relatively competent investigation rather than on pleasant theorizing, albeit on inquiry into self-reported and/or obviously subjective human experiences.

All that we can "know" of death is what we can observe in those who are dying and what we hear from those who have been close to death. Lore has it that persons near death frequently experience visions—or, if one prefers, accurate perceptions of what lies beyond. It is folk wisdom that persons who are drowning see their lives "flash before them" and so on. Yet, apparently the first systematic effort to investigate deathbed visions was undertaken in the 1920s by an Irish physicist, William Barrett. Barrett became so intrigued by the tale of a woman who, shortly before death, spoke intensely of a vision of "lovely brightness" and of the presence of her dead father and sister, and implied a pleasurable sense of being drawn away from life, that he collected a number of such cases and published them in 1926. In 1959, a psychologist with special interest in extrasensory perception, Karlis Osis, contacted 10,000 physicians and nurses and received questionnaire replies from 6% of them, reporting over 35,000 observations of death experiences. In 2% of these cases, elevated mood prior to death was reported; in 3% of the deaths there were indications that patients had seen visions; and in 4% of the cases apparitions had seemingly appeared to the dying persons. In-depth follow-up investigations were conducted in some 200 of these cases (135). Later, between 1961 and 1964, Osis obtained data on about 50,000 dying persons in and around the state of New York, reported by 20% of a random sample of 5000 physicians and nurses in that area who responded to a questionnaire study. Still later, in 1972–1973, Osis and his phychologist colleague, Haraldsson, investigated deathbed phenomena in India so that cross-cultural data might be developed. An interview technique was subsequently pursued with selected cases (136). While the eventual follow-up data on about 1000 instances of death and near death show that deathbed visions seem actually to be rare—on an order apparently involving only 2% to 4% of dying persons—the Osis–Haraldsson analysis of events which seem to occur among those few make for fascinating reading and speculation. The student of thanatology or of lamentology should do both, starting with the Osis–Haraldsson book, *At the Hour of Death*, published in 1977. Perhaps the most striking feature of this work is the statistical objectivity of complex interaction analysis and intellectual skepticism which its authors have brought to a task which virtually defies conventional scientific method.

At about the same time that Osis and Haraldsson were tramping through Northern India inquiring into deathbed apparitions and mood elevations, an investigation with broader implications was going on in the United States, which has resulted in the construction of a theoretical model of experiences which may be common to some persons as they face death.

Having earned a Ph.D. in philosophy, Raymond A. Moody is a scholar in the classic sense. In an effort to pursue his area of particular interest, the philosophy of medicine, Moody later attended medical school and subsequently became a student of psychiatry. Quite by accident, he encountered a few people, unknown to each other, who in the course of conversation reported that they had at past times in their lives been near death—and that during the condition they had experienced phenomena of sight and sound which struck Moody by their remarkable similarity. These are persons of a sort which Osis and Haraldsson have called "come-back cases" (137). Moody was able to identify about 150 persons who had been near death, and undertook to interview some 50 of these individuals regarding their mental experiences while in the near-death state.

Moody reports that, for the most part, his subjects were persons who had been "thought, adjudged, or pronounced clinically dead" and were resuscitated, or "who, in the course of accidents or severe injury or illness, came very close to physical death" (138). Some of the events described were quite recent and others relatively old. A few reports were apparently secondhand, coming from persons who were in communication with others when they died.

Moody's findings have been reported in his book, *Life After Life*. The Moody inquiries, as he is careful to point out, are not in the nature of scientific investigation in any pure sense; his cases are not, nor are they represented as being, a random sample (in fact, he seems to have stumbled across most of them very casually). Various desirable controls have not been introduced; no cross-cultural cases are represented. His technique has been one of interviewing some people who nearly died. Still, the astonishing similarities among reports given by Moody's few subjects (who are unlikely to have influenced each other's revelations) give reason to believe that similar phenomena may be experienced by some persons who are close to clinical death and who are later revived.

Moody reports in those he interviewed that no two of their stories were precisely identical although a few are "remarkably close" to being identical. Further, no one person has reported *each* of the various components of the near-death experience, and no single element of the composite has been reported by each subject (although some elements are "close" to being universal). Of the elements supplied by the researcher as being typical, none has been reported by only one of his respondents but has shown up "many" different times. A "few" people reported none of the elements and were amnesic for events of their "deaths," or they reported absence of memory for any such events.

While the order of experienced components may differ, Moody says that wide variations from the sequence were unusual. "In general, persons who were 'dead' seem to report more florid, complete experiences than those who only came close to death, and those who were 'dead' for a longer period go deeper than those who were 'dead' for a shorter time" (139).

Reports provided by the subjects characterized their experiences as being unsuited for clear reporting in available language; Moody describes these experiences as having a quality of ineffability or of inexpressibility. Yet, respondents were careful to distinguish between the events in which they had participated and the experience of dreaming or fantasizing; they describe their experiences as being "definitely, emphatically real."

Reported Components of the Death Experience

Ten specific elements of the "model near-death experience" are given here, having been condensed from the Moody report, provided more thoroughly and with interesting discussion in *Life After Life*. Again, the sequence is typical but not universal, and not all persons experienced each event.

1. The person hears himself pronounced dead. According to Moody, "numerous" people have heard their deaths pronounced by persons in the immediate environment (140).

> I arrested on them. I heard the radiologist . . . say, "Dr. James, I've killed your patient" . . . and I knew I wasn't dead. I tried to move or to let them know, but I couldn't. When they were trying to resuscitate me, I could hear them telling how many c.c.'s of something to give me, but I didn't feel the needle going in. I felt nothing at all when they touched me.

2. The person experiences intense feelings of peace. Persons who were near death from various causes have remarked as follows on their states of mind after hearing themselves pronounced dead: "I couldn't feel a thing in the world except peace, comfort, ease—just quietness." "All I felt was warmth and the most extreme comfort I have ever experienced."

3. The person begins to hear a noise. Moody says that the noise has been described as "a roaring, a banging, and as a whistling sound, like the wind" (141). Other examples include the following: "A really bad buzzing noise coming from inside my head"; "an annoying buzzing, ringing sound"; "a loud ringing; it could be described as a buzzing"; "I began to hear music of some sort, a majestic, really beautiful sort of music."

4. *There is a sensation of being alone in a tunnel.* Moody reports that he has "heard this space described as a cave, a well, a trough, an enclosure, a tunnel, a funnel, a vacuum, a void, a sewer, a valley, and a cylinder" (142).

> I found myself in a tunnel—a tunnel of concentric circles.
>
> I entered head-first into a narrow and very, very dark passageway. I seemed to just fit inside of it. I began to slide down, down, down.
>
> I felt that I was in a private world.
>
> I was desperately alone. (143)

5. *One has a sense of moving through the tunnel.* The Moody subjects have made comments about their sensations in the "tunnel" as follows: "I felt as if I were moving in a vacuum, just through blackness"; "I had the feeling that I was moving through a very deep, very dark valley"; "I went through this dark, black vacuum at super speed." Osis and Haraldsson report dying patients' experiences of seeming to be transported elsewhere in an environment of "bright, saturated colors, peace, harmony and extraordinary beauty."

6. *The person sees his own body, as from a distance, and observes others attempting to revive him.* Among the most interesting reports provided by Moody in *Life After Life* are those in which persons who have experienced near death have had perceptions of being weightless spectators at events surrounding themselves in their near-death situation. One said, "It seemed as if I were a spectator rather than that person—that body—they were working on." Another reported, "I was out of my body looking at it from about ten yards away," while another implied fluctuation between living and dying: "I kept getting in and

out of my physical body, and I could see it from directly above." Moody says that a number of physicians have told him "that they are utterly baffled about how patients with no medical knowledge could describe in such detail and so correctly the procedures used in resuscitation attempts."

In the near-death episodes, "Physical objects present no barrier" to the individual who is experiencing these events, Moody reports. "Movement from one place to another can be extremely rapid, almost instantaneous." One participant in the study said that she "went out of her body and into another room in the hospital where she found her older sister crying and saying, "Oh, Kathy, please don't die, please don't die." The older sister was quite baffled when, later, Kathy told her exactly where she had been and what she had been saying during this time."

7. *Others come to interact with the person; often these are relatives and friends known to be already dead.* Moody says that "quite a few" of his subjects reported other "spiritual . . . beings who apparently were there to ease them through their transition into death, or in two cases to tell them that their time to die had not yet come and that they must return to their physical bodies" (144). (Osis and Haraldsson report similar episodes of such otherworldly rejection.)

According to Moody, more than a mere presence of such "spirits" has been suggested. "A woman told me that as she was leaving her body she detected the presence of two other spiritual beings there, and that they identified themselves as her 'spiritual helpers' " (145). Another said, "I felt they had come to protect me or to guide me," and still another said, "Whenever I wondered what was going on, I would always get a thought back from one of them, that everything was all right, that I was dying but would be fine."

Osis and Haraldsson have made a distinction between the visions of dying persons who were otherwise fully conscious, in good psychological contact with their environments and apparently well-oriented, and the hallucinations

of persons in obvious emotional distress caused by psychopathology, brain trauma, high fevers, or medications with
hallucinogenic effects (146). In the former cases, visions
were overwhelmingly of close, dead relatives possessing
clear but gently persuasive and acceptable "take-away"
motives, whereas the latter cases were characterized by
"this world" hallucinations of "strangers or bizarre char-
acters" who were, normally, alive or thought to be alive,
or "replays of this world memories." Persons in good physical health who experience hallucinations seem to halluci-
nate the dead and "other world" phenomena (147). Imag-
ery involving "other world" figures seemed to stimulate
"peace, serenity, and joy" (148), and "spirit guides" were
seen, at least by American respondents in the Osis–
Haraldsson study, as "friendly and understanding" (149),
in one case as a beautiful room full of people waiting in
greeting (150). When apparitions were seen by dying persons, they were "nearly always" believed to be "messengers
from a postmortem form of existence," whose gratifying
purposes were clearly of a take-away nature (151).

    *8. A shapeless but personable "being of light" appears,
offering unconditional positive regard.* Moody reveals that
to those who have perceived the being of light, its description is utterly invariable. Moody says that "typically, at
its first appearance, this light is dim, but it rapidly gets
brighter until it reaches an unearthly brilliance." The light
is reported as being of a white or clear quality, but it is not
in any way hurtful, nor is it a death personification in the
form of a skeleton or other spectral figure, although it may
be given religious interpretation (152, 153). Moody quotes
a respondent: "It was this huge beam. It was just a tremendous amount of light, nothing like a big bright flash-
light. It was just too much light. And it gave off heat to
me; I felt a warm sensation."

    Apparently sounds do not come from the "being."
Moody reports his respondents as having said that "Direct,
unimpeded transfer of thought takes place, and in such a

clear way that there is no possibility whatsoever either of misunderstanding or of lying to the light.''

Osis and Haraldsson report that 62% of the patients whose records they studied died within a day of perceiving the apparition, and that more than a quarter died within an hour (154). For most, unconsciousness followed quickly upon interaction with the apparition.

9. The "being of light" invites the person to review his life, and a playback of events in the person's life occurs. Moody says that reports exist in which "the review is experienced even though the being of light does not appear," and that it is "often obvious that the being can see the individual's whole life displayed and that he doesn't need the information. His only intention is to provoke reflection" (155). Persons are encouraged by the "being of light" to think about their lives, to examine their works and readiness for death—but not in an accusatory or threatening way, for persons "still feel the total love and acceptance coming from the light, no matter what their answers might be." These life reviews are, according to Osis and Haraldsson (156), without elements of judgment, salvation or redemption. Visions of hell or of devils are "almost totally absent." The life review is rapid, and, according to Moody, "incredibly vivid and real." Moody does not say how many cases of life review were reported by those who provided his data; "very few" such cases were found by Osis in his 1959 study. The panoramic memory was not investigated by Osis and Haraldsson in their later work since "panoramic memory recall also occurs in other situations not just in patients who are near death" (157).

10. A representation of a dividing line between life and death appears. The "border" experience is reported as occuring in a "few" instances, and, in Moody's experience, has been represented as "a body of water, a gray mist, a door, a fence . . . or simply a line" (158).

> I saw a fence. I started moving toward the fence, and I saw
> a man on the other side of it, moving toward it as if to meet
> me. I wanted to reach him, but I felt myself being drawn
> back, irresistibly. As I did, I saw him, too, turn around and
> go back in the other direction.

> I looked up and said, "Lord, here I am. If you want me,
> take me." Boy, he shot me back so fast it felt like I almost
> lost my breath.

The phenomenon has been reported elsewhere as a
"golden light" across a river and as bridges to another
shore (159). Osis and Haraldsson believe that deathbed
visions are of short duration, with about 50% lasting 5
minutes or less and about 80% lasting less than an hour
(160).

Speculation

There is a terrific temptation to speculate about these
reports and what they may mean, and the reader probably
will not be quite comfortable for awhile until he does so.
In addition, though, some of the present writer's thoughts
may be in order—with considerable restraint and all
modesty—for whatever stimulus they might provide, as
all of us with interest in various aspects of life consider
these newly reported episodes relating to dying and death.

All kinds of explanations come to mind as to why the
"Moody Effect" may happen, but the explanations are
not important except perhaps in some abstract sense of
knowing for the joy of knowing. What *is* important is that
the Moody Effect *seems to happen* with some people who
are near death and who recover.

Since our purpose here is to consider ways in which persons might be helped in prebereavement and in grief, it
would perhaps be useful to suggest to such persons when a
death is imminent that "Soon your loved person will experience profound peace; he will be aware of your close-

ness and deep concern, but he will also be experiencing others who have been close to him and have died. Your loved person will then have a sense of being in a warm and compassionate presence, and in that presence he'll review his life before he finds that he must cross the border and leave you here for awhile."

But can we say this, or something like it, truthfully?

Does the Moody Effect happen to people who are experiencing death?

Actually, anything we "know" is merely a sensory experience. The table is "there" only because we perceive it as being real, and so on. Moody's subjects "know" that certain events have transpired in their near-deaths; they reject any idea that they were hallucinating (of course hallucinations, by definition, *seem terribly real*), as Moody, Osis and Haraldsson reject the idea that these sensory adventures are stimulated by drugs, oxygen deprivation, loneliness, projection, schizoid reaction, neurologic dysfunction, or the like. In fact, in the Osis and Haraldsson studies, 80% of subjects were persons who had either received no medicine at all or such low levels of medication that psychological influence was unlikely. Over 90% had either normal temperatures or only mild fevers (161).

It seems clear that during near-death a variety of things are happening to a person's physical and psychological mechanisms which have not occurred for that person in the same combination before and that, therefore, the sensations which are recalled upon recovery or which are enacted before death must be interpreted intellectually by a system of reasoning which is unpracticed in dealing with similar stimuli. Possibly the closest way to understand and interpret these stimuli is to cast them in concepts which are widely recognized and common to all as theoretical or religious or philosophical or "folk" components of the death experience.

But again, these thoughts in and of themselves are worthless if they are to serve as partial explanations, because explanations of *why* are unimportant to the pragmatist *if* the

Moody Effect occurs in people who are experiencing death. *If* the effect happens, it *happens*.

> *None cometh from thence*
> *That he may tell us how they fare.*
> SONG OF THE HARP PLAYER
> (ABOUT 2100 BC)

The difficulty is that we do not know what thoughts people have as they experience death. We are not sure whether, as death occurs, comatose people have any thoughts at all, and there is at least the possibility that in the profoundly depressed physical/psychological state which must characterize much dying, nothing occurs which we would understand as thinking, awareness, or cognitive management of events in the environment—even though in half of the Osis and Haraldsson cases, persons were fully conscious and aware at the time visions occurred (162). At best, what we have are the characterizations of unusual stimuli as provided by a few persons who have been very close to death and who have recovered to sort out, process, and recount their interpretations of unusual sensory experiences, and by persons who have died and whose unusual behaviors and comments have been repeated for us by others who were there. We have no reports of people who have experienced "life after life," since the only first-hand reports are not those of persons who were once dead but only of persons who were erroneously declared so.

Does the Moody Effect happen, *without sufficient recovery to permit the intellectual activity necessary* to interpret environmental and intrapsychological events associated with the final stages of clinical death?

We do not yet know what happens as people experience death. We have reports only on interpretations provided by some few who have recovered from *near*-death and from others who have observed deaths and who have reported on what they think was happening with a small percentage of others. That information is important in its own right, but it can be taken no further. The only possible tentative conclusion, important though it may be, is that some persons who have been close to death interpret their sensory experiences with remarkable similarity.

We cannot know if sensory phenomena in near-death and in death are similar until our own turns come. If, then, we enjoy the Moody Effect and are drawn to the other side—as a final thought, we can only then exclaim "Aha!"

> *To die will be an awfully*
> *big adventure.*
>
> *J. M. BARRIE*
> *PETER PAN*

II

✧✦✧·✦✧

GRIEVING

✧✦✧·✦✧

cA s children, we all had fantasies of abandonment.
Now, when a person close to us dies, those early
fantasies are confirmed. A number of psychoanalysts have
argued for years that grief experiences begin during the
first year of life, when babies are weaned and experience
separation anxiety or something very much like it (163). Is
it any wonder, then, that the feelings are so distressing?

> *It is the peculiarity of grief to*
> *bring out the childish side of man.*
> *VICTOR HUGO*
> *LES MISERABLES*

   Grief is not an illness. One who is experiencing it will
very likely feel awful, but the pain is not caused by an in-
fection curable by drugs, a breakage open to remedy by
splints, or the malfunctioning of some organ which can be
repaired surgically. Grief is not a medical condition, it is a
psychological one, and relief from its frequently agonizing
symptoms lies in our individual psychologies, in the emo-

tional environments in which we find our support, and in the passage of time.

Grief is a typical reaction to the death of some close and perhaps loved person. Grief reactions—or feelings which are so much like grief reactions that they might as well be called that—are common also in response to human events and experiences other than death. Divorce (the death of a relationship) would be one example, particularly in those divorces in which at least one partner retains the love relationship and does not want to be separated—divorce is now replacing death as the major cause of marital disruption (164). Another example would be abortion; a grief response to spontaneous abortion (miscarriage) is very common, and is not unheard of following induced abortion (165). Still other stimuli which provoke grief responses include personal separations (166), retirement, or the loss of an important job (167), leaving one school for another, moving from a familiar neighborhood, the breaking off of a romantic relationship, amputation (168) and mastectomy, giving up infants for adoption, loss of valued property, or organ dysfunction (169). The person who suffers a stroke and later experiences reduced function (paralysis, brain damage, loss of some other ability) may also grieve.

We can begin our process of understanding by defining three terms which are often used interchangeably but which technically have quite different meanings.

First, there is *bereavement*. Bereavement has to do with the time at which a significant death occurs, so one can speak of events which are prebereavement or of events which are postbereavement and make sense in a time frame relative to whether or not someone has died.

The term *grief*, on the other hand, normally implying acute grief as opposed to that which is chronic and unusually long-lasting, has to do with the feeling experience of deep and sometimes violent sorrow, of altered mood and affect appropriate to the death of a loved person. Grief is an emotional and behavioral reaction which happens when a love tie is severed. The sense of loss is real. So in the idea of grief we are not talking about the deep melancholia and despair of a depression (which may have no clear and obvious cause) but of a reaction to some actual and significant emotional loss.

In *Henry IV* Shakespeare referred to "a plague of sighing and grief," and in 1944 the psychotherapist Lindemann expanded the germ of this idea to provide the classic definition of acute grief as a syndrome:

> sensations of somatic distress occurring in waves lasting from twenty minutes to an hour at a time, a feeling of tightness in the throat, choking with shortness of breath, need for sighing, and an empty feeling in the abdomen, lack of muscular power, and an intense subjective distress described as tension or mental pain.

Lindemann's work was based on observations of reactions to the death of victims of the Coconut Grove fire in Boston, of military persons killed during wartime, and of individuals who died while some friend with a psychoneurotic difficulty was in treatment, so its broad applicability must be regarded as open to the findings of controlled research investigation. However, Lindemann was among the first, and later studies have shown that despite the heavy traumatic bias of his observations they were remarkably close to what has been observed more recently.

Grief is commonly experienced as prebereavement, by both the survivors and by the dying person himself; and it usually lasts for some little while after a death has occurred. A time period of about a year for completion of the deep acute grief process is often mentioned, but Carey found depression in a quarter of the persons he interviewed 12 months after their bereavements (170), and some parents whose children have died report that the second postbereavement year was actually their most difficult. The variations in both duration and severity of a bereavement reaction seem to have a good deal to do with how successfully one handles what Freud (171) and many others have called "grief work" (172-174). One who *wishes* to remember will never forget, and a person who has experienced the death of someone who was loved will never "get over" it in the sense of forgetting. In some instances one's grief work may never be completed (175), particularly if one is not prepared to give it the difficult and demanding intellectual and emotional effort which grief work requires (176). However, the initial awful grief seems to be limited to the first few weeks, and subsequent heavy grief, with some variations and allowances for differing circumstances, tends in most cases to diminish markedly after a year or so, after the person arrives at what de Molina calls "internal acceptance" which is quite different from the "external acceptance" of reality, which occurs much earlier (177).

> It can be at least two years to begin to find a new direction—
> to begin to accommodate. Every bereaved person knows
> this. He also knows that the outsider who is not bereaved
> often does not comprehend or have patience with the ex-
> tent of his grief and the degree to which his life is dis-
> rupted and must be rebuilt. (178)

The passage of time may be the most important factor in resolution of grief (179). But time only heals, it does not erase. As Cicero pointed out, "There is no grief which does not lessen and soften," and in time the sensation will be that of the curtains beginning to open and sunlight coming through again.

It is the grief of surviving persons that will be central to these discussions of the grief syndrome—the grief of those who live on (and a death rarely affects only the immediate family and friendship circle; a death extends far beyond to include many persons who touch and have been touched by this person and this family). But we must not lose sight of the fact that the dying need to do their own grieving, even if it is true in most cases that persons other than ourselves will normally be the ones to take primary care of the moribund.

Then, we have the word *mourning*. Mourning means only the expression of sorrow, what Engel (180) has called the *process*; the individual is doing those things which in his particular culture indicate that he is going through a grief process. In 1917, Freud was using the word mourning to mean what is now called grief—except, perhaps, by the more entrenched psychoanalysts. Freud was interested in mourning as it related to melancholia, a thought which was first explored by Freud's student, Karl Abraham, in 1912. But the distinctions between grief and mourning are only semantic for practical purposes. The distinction is made here so that the two ideas can be discussed without their being mutually confusing. Grief is the affective experience, mourning is its social expression.

Grief is a normal response to a particular kind of stress. Most people, sooner or later, experience it. Virtually all people will be in a position at one time or another to assist others with their grief processes in response to death—two thirds of the time of someone over 65 years old, one third of the time to the death of someone younger (181).

Despite the fact that grief is the only emotional difficulty the cause of which is obvious, the distinctive features of which are recognized, and the prognosis for which is highly predictable (182), the study of this psychological process is new. Though the idea of "grief work" was discussed by Freud as early as 1917, in 1972 the British psychiatrist, Parkes, was complaining that grief as a topic is rarely listed in the indexes of textbooks in psychiatry. Parkes has turned out to be one of a relatively few people who have tried to do something about that deficiency, and today he ranks as one of the few good researchers who have helped our understanding of how to assist bereaved persons by understanding first what is happening with them.

Most psychiatric "research" on grief must be regarded as weak, if understandably so, when standards of research in psychology and professional counseling are applied. Research in grief is based largely on subjective clinical observations, retrospective reconstructions, impressions, opinions, case histories, and interesting theorizing. Much of it is simply the report of this psychiatrist or that one who had a bereaved patient and wrote an article about his experiences with that person or who has offered comment on some other therapist's case report. Psychologists specializing in psychotherapy are infrequently heard from on the topic of therapy for bereavement, and only very recently have journals addressed to professional counselors given attention to what bereavement is about. The observations of these highly trained and skilled contemporary professionals are not particularly improved, except in clarity of language, from what the poets were saying centuries ago. Isaiah, Homer, Sophocles, and Euripides were among the early commentators, not to mention vintage observers like Shakespeare who also understood the meaning of grief, or "new boys" like A. E. Housman:

> *With rue my heart is laden*
> *For golden friends I had,*
> *For many a rose-lipt maiden*
> *And many a lightfoot lad.*
> *By brooks too broad for leaping*
> *The lightfoot boys are laid;*
> *The rose-lipt girls are sleeping*
> *In fields where roses fade.*
>
> *A SHROPSHIRE LAD*

Yet today, even as George Engel was saying in 1964, there remains a "dearth of systematic knowledge, much less scientific study, of the process of grief and mourning," although it can be noted gratifyingly that there have been a number of doctoral dissertations directed toward these phenomena, particularly since the mid-1970s.

GRIEF AS A PROCESS

Operating from theory which evolved from his clinical work, which led to interest in what he called (and distinguished between) "mourning and melancholia," Freud described four major characteristics of the syndrome: profoundly painful dejection, cessation of interest in the outside world, loss of capacity to love, and inhibition of activity. Freud believed that a capacity for love (loosely, *libido*) goes from one's self outward to others, and that the loss of an important "other" has the effect of liberating the libido, which can then attach to some other person or persons ("object") or can center again, as in infancy, on the self. This process is what Freud believed was central to what he called mourning (183).

Much more recently Parkes has emerged as among the most notable of researchers investigating postbereavement grief in a systematic way (184). Basing his findings on the reported experiences of a number of British widows (185) and patients in psychiatric hospitals (186), he tells us that grief is not a fixed state (187), but rather it is a process; it is not a set of symptoms which start with bereavement and then gradually fade away but a succession of clinical pictures which blend into one another, replace one another, and recur from time to time in overlapping patterns. Parkes believes that while there is a pattern, the stages are not necessarily sequential and are not clear-cut. There *is* a pattern, and it holds up pretty well, but parts of the pattern appear at different times, under different conditions; thus, the grief syndrome is not so much a matter of letting psychological events take place in a known and predetermined order as it is of expecting their appearance in a predictable sequence but anticipating too that parts of that pattern may occur nonsequentially. The grief syndrome is full of remissions and relapses, but as a general rule it can be expected that persons will cope with bereavement with the same psychological mechanisms they have employed previously to contend with other life stresses. The feelings must be "worked through," for if they were to be confronted directly, and all at once, they could prove overwhelming (188).

THE GRIEVING FEELING

When a death occurs, "The smooth, more or less automatic, taken for granted aspects of living are interrupted" (189). Perhaps humans find security in stability, and any change in the environment affects stability and, from that, security, with the greatest threat to security following from the most impactful environmental changes. Whether or not this speculation is accurate, Parkes says that the grief which follows is such a powerful reaction that for a time it overshadows all other sources of difficulty (190). The experience resembles a physical injury, one's "self" has been hurt; it will be spoken of as a "blow," there has been a functional wound; the injury heals gradually, but occasionally there will be some complication which will reopen the wound, and, as is true with physical injuries, when this happens the healing process seems to take longer (191).

> Object loss may be compared to a wound and mourning to wound healing. Like wound healing, successful mourning involves an orderly sequence and an irreducible interval of time, interference with which may distort the process of healing and lead to pathological consequences. And, like wound healing, pre-existing and previous conditions will influence or change the course of the process and sometimes prevent it altogether (192).

When it is a beloved and intimate
human being that is dying, besides

> *the horror at the extinction of life*
> *there is a severance, a spiritual*
> *wound, which like a physical wound*
> *is sometimes fatal and sometimes*
> *heals.*
>
> *TOLSTOY*

As Nichols and Nichols have suggested, grief work must be attended to, and it is far better in the long run to get battered and bruised in the game than to simply sit in the bleachers and intellectualize (193); we cannot cure our emotional hurts by hiding them, since they cannot be hidden well or successfully, and it is far better for even psychological wounds to be open and healing than closed and festering.

Grief may not stimulate the sort of pain which can be described as readily as a physical hurt, but the poignant aching can be acutely unpleasant, and it usually interferes with the ways in which a person feels, thinks and acts. That explains why newly bereaved persons are commonly treated as if they were ill, why the bereaved person is expected to be absent from his job and to stay home; that is why visitors address him with hushed voices and why the individual may wonder later, in all sincerity, how it was that he ever lived through the first several days (194). One simply cannot "pick up the pieces and go on" instantly—a piece is now missing.

Parkes points out that time is uncertain to the bereaved person. Later on the first postbereavement year may be remembered as a kind of jumble of senseless activity, although perceptions of the dead person may be extraordinarily clear and well defined.

> *She, she is dead; she's dead; when*
> *thou know'st this,*

> *Thou know'st how dry a cinder*
> *this world is.*
>
> *JOHN DONNE*
> *THE FIRST ANNIVERSARY*

When we think about how best to help grieving people, probably the most important thing for us to keep in mind is that mourning and the expression of grief are psychological necessities—they are not contemptible weaknesses or self-indulgences (195); they are necessities. This fact is recognized in Jewish tradition, which requires prompt burial, acceptance of the reality, and open expression of sorrow. The tradition expects 3 days of deep grief, 7 days of mourning, 30 days of gradual readjustment, and 11 months of remembrance and healing.

It is accepted, too, that people will express grief in a variety of ways and that no one way is best, insofar as is now known (196). Crying and sobbing are common, and it is the reaction one expects to see among most persons, in the early days especially, but other people will react in different ways, probably in much the same ways that they have handled previous life stresses. Regardless of how a person manages his grief, the important thing is that his feelings be allowed to emerge, to be acknowledged and worked through and not suppressed. Grief is like any other strong feeling; if it is bottled up it will cause trouble.

According to Parkes grief may take various forms: it can be prompt or delayed—sometimes its expression may be unusual, and occasionally the symptoms that are usually transient and not especially troublesome can cause deeply profound distress (197). A number of things determine how a person will react to bereavement: age, personality factors and predispositions to emotional stress, opportunity to prepare for bereavement (little warning can prognosticate poor bereavement outcome), genetic givens, previous life experiences and successes in working through those which were difficult, socioeconomic status, satisfaction in the marital relationship, available cultural and psychological support systems, and so on—but the process is normal and necessary (198). Parkes has classified these as determinants which are *antecedant* to the death (such as previous deep losses), concurrent with (e.g., inhibition of strong affect) or *subsequent* to it (as, for example, psychological support or emotional isolation) (199).

Another factor may relate to the psychological status of the patient at the time of his death; assumptions have been made that the comatose patient or person who can't communicate because of stroke or other trauma will become "socially dead" to his family more quickly than will the dying patient who can communicate (200, 201).

One doesn't have to show intense and prolonged grief to demonstrate his true love for some dead person; one doesn't have to seek out a psychologist or counselor's therapeutic intervention to prove unending devotion, although some people can well use this special kind of assistance if it helps with the grief (as distinguished from the individual who seeks therapy to show everyone how sorry he is). Virtually everyone who is undergoing the grief experience could probably be helped by someone who is familiar with what the grief process is all about and who is trained and experienced in therapies related to bereavement, but the point to remember is that the seeking of special professional help should be encouraged only when there is belief that it will help the bereaved person get his life back in order more comfortably, and not simply to provide evidence for others that his heartbreak would otherwise be unendurable.

EXPRESSION

The individual's reaction in a time of grief will depend in large measure on how the various predisposing factors are arrayed and how they operate together. If we can assume a Gestalt, we can also assume that the whole will be

greater than the sum of its parts, and that is why grief reactions can be so varied among individuals, even while the
basic pattern seems to be present in all cases.

Parkes has identified and described three basic patterns
of grief reaction, and virtually everyone will fit one of those
patterns as best we now understand the complex processes
of human grieving (202).

Prompt Emotionality

The first pattern, which we call *prompt emotionality*, is
one of severe disturbance of emotionality and affect occurring within a week of bereavement, with the disturbance
remaining through the first month and through much of
the second, but with a rapid tapering off followed by only
mild disturbances of emotionality during the third month
and thereafter. According to Parkes, widows who are most
distressed at first recover more quickly than those who
show little initial emotion (203).

Second Week Emotionality

We call the second pattern *second week emotionality*.
It includes moderate emotionality in the first week, with
severely disturbed affect in the second week, followed by
rapid recovery.

Delayed Emotionality

In the third pattern, *delayed emotionality*, little or no
emotion occurs during the first postbereavement week, as
grieving is avoided; but by the fourth week, moderate disturbances of emotionality appear, and moderate to severe
disturbances show up at about 3 months postbereavement,
with significantly more disturbance than one sees in either
of the first two patterns (204, 205). When delayed emotionality is being exhibited, there will be improvement
after the profound upset at 3 months, but there will be a

terrific relapse at about the time of the first anniversary of the death. The people who fall into this third pattern, according to Parkes, seem to be younger than the others, and the pattern seems more often than not to have followed a sudden death. Beyond that, these relatively young people who are responding to the sudden death of a loved person often have histories of previous emotional distress. Their postbereavement pattern is one of avoiding grief expression or acceptance of sorrow, even to the extent of abstaining from the most usual sorts of formal mourning, and staying away from the cemetery except perhaps for the funeral. They typically display a pattern of staying extraordinarily busy, apparently in order to avoid the terribly strong feelings which they are suppressing. These are the ones who turn up with the profound reaction at 3 months and the shattering relapse on the first anniversary. It is interesting to notice, too, the Parkes research finding that people who fall into this third pattern are persons who were showing their grief during the first month by having lots of physical symptoms, probably psychosomatic, significantly more than those complained of by people who "break down" during the first week of bereavement. They can even experience loss of hair, which is not at all common among persons exhibiting the first two types of grief pattern. Furthermore, the overall emotional adjustment of people in the third pattern after 13 months is poor relative to the others, and virtually all of the members of the third group have psychological difficulties of one sort or another. This is not necessarily because of faulty handling of grief, because it should be remembered that people who follow the third pattern seem to be people who, for the most part, had psychological difficulties before the death, too.

A psychiatrist (206) has had this to say about delayed grief:

> The patient who, at the moment of the loss, appeared to be unaffected, at some later time may suddenly develop feel-

ings of grief which are uncontrollable. We find such delayed grief reactions in people whose attitudes toward objects they mourn had always been ambivalent. The delayed reaction is usually the result of a resurgence of guilt feelings.*

Another observer has pointed out:

> Sometimes, the initial response is overtly an intellectual acceptance of the reality of the loss and an immediate initiation of apparently appropriate activity, such as making arrangements and comforting others. But it is only by not permitting access to consciousness of the full emotional impact of the loss that this can take place. In such an instance, the loss is recognized but its painful character is denied or at least muted. (207)

Elsewhere, Engel said:

> The survivor may minimize the effect of the loss, which instead is projected onto another mutual mourner, for whom he may feel sorry. In addition, the other mourner is taken as a replacement object who is unrealistically expected to fulfill the role of the lost-object. If this is done at the expense of the work of grief, a depressive response may develop at some later date, as when the vicarious object disappoints or leaves. Following this, the survivor may fall ill. (208)

This kind of vicarious displacement and absorption in caring for other bereaved persons can sometimes amount to compulsion, according to Bowlby (209).

There is no question that delayed grief is far more painful than that which is managed relatively promptly, and the fact suggests that the helper could be useful by encouraging early grief expression to help persons "take the pain hard and fast" (210), but one must be careful here. One

---

*From "Reactive Depression," by Emil A. Guthiel, in the AMERICAN HANDBOOK OF PSYCHIATRY, First Edition, Volume 1, edited by Silvano Arieti, (C) 1959 by Basic Books, Inc., Publishers, New York.

must keep in mind the wide range of human differences in potential emotional response; those who, for their own and perhaps unshared psychological reasons, need to delay the grief should not be forced into what the helper may see as more appropriate earlier grief work. Such a course can lead to more harm than good.

"Women usually come out of bereavement worse than men," at least in the short term (211, 212). A much higher percentage of them wind up in psychiatric hospitals; more of them consult counselors; they consume more sedatives and tranquilizers; they exhibit more distress following bereavement. Yet, in the long run, perhaps 2 to 4 years post-bereavement, it is the men who seem to take longer to fully recover. As we know, men are culturally conditioned to inhibit the emotional responses which are more readily available to women, and this may be another area in which the socially imposed "strength demand" takes its toll on men. Yet, a very similar attitude may beset women. Pomeroy found that widows commonly "split off" the necessary content of those things which must be done here and now and repress the affect, apparently trying unconsciously to "tuck the pain away" (213).

MEANINGS OF A DEATH IN THE FAMILY

The loss of a husband or wife is one of the most severe forms of psychological stress; the same can be said of the loss of any person who is especially close. This is particularly true when the death is sudden or accidental and when it involves a person in the prime of life, which can be defined as any time prior to senescence (214–216). Fulton and Fulton tell us that parent responses to infant death can be especially profound (217). The grief response to a stillbirth is likely to be less intense than response to death of a child who has lived as long as a day. "Affectional bonding" seems to begin before a mother has physical contact with her newly born child and prior to the time she gives it care; both contact and caring increase the bonding and thus increase the grief level when children survive their birth only to die soon after (218). Some parents will deliberately conceive while an existing child is fatally ill so that a "replacement" will be available, and cases have been reported in which the mothers in these circumstances have, in the absence of therapeutic support, experienced resultant confusion, guilt, severe depression, and ambivalence (219). (For an extended discussion of nursing care for bereaved parents see Seitz and Warrick [220].) Yet another occasional response is "scapegoating," in which parental frustration following a child's death is taken out on some surviving child or children (221).

The predominating life stresses of women during terminal illness of a husband center on family life changes (222). Chaplain Kermit Smith, of Kansas City, Missouri's Research Medical Center, believes that humans experience possessiveness of one another, and that the greater the possessiveness, the greater the postbereavement grief. The notion is consistent with Bowlby's view that unduly strong possessiveness, in combination with anger for the lost love object, sets up ambivalence in the relationship, which is the basis for guilt in bereavement (223). Parkes has approached this idea from a somewhat different angle, proposing that the amount of stress which can be expected in bereavement seems to have a lot to do with how much of each other's *life spaces* the dead person and the survivor have occupied (224). The greater the life space occupancy the higher the *grief potential*, to use Fulton and Fulton's term (225); the less the life space occupancy the less the grief potential. The more Person A has invested in the life of Person B, the higher the potential is for a deep grief reaction to the death of Person B. (See Figure 1.) There will be a kind of psychological dismemberment, an emotional amputation, an affective tearing asunder; thus, a high grief potential.

The life space idea has been important to Parkes, but Freud couched basically the same ideas in his terms of libidinal attachments, hypercathexis, and other psychoana-

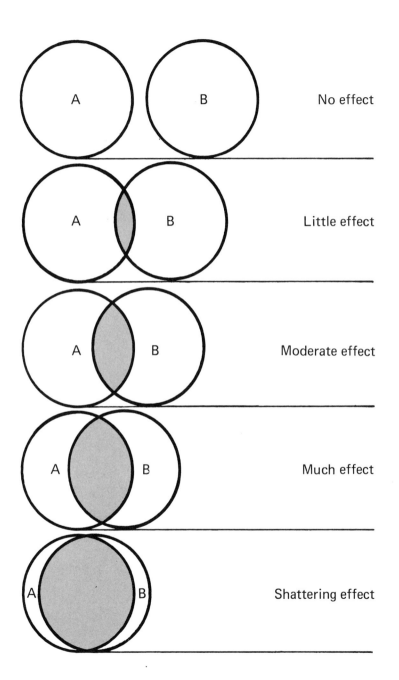

lytic formulations (226). Much more recently a very important dissertation on the same theme has been offered by Schor who asserts that as humans we structure our existence in terms of various cognitive dimensions, central to which are core elements, principally our relationships with significant others (227). When death takes such a significant other, a traumatic disruption of our *core* occurs, by which we are damaged and reduced temporarily to less adequate methods of coping, with disruption of cognitive, somatic, affective, and behavioral functioning.

Western societies are characterized in part by small family units (228), and the elderly are largely segregated from the emotional lives of their families and the social lives of their communities (229), making their deaths, typically, ones of relatively low grief potential. Within this structure, dependent children and their parents occupy enormous areas of each other's life spaces, and the life spaces of wives are conventionally more heavily occupied by their husbands than wives are conventionally invested in the life spaces of their husbands (230).

Prince Albert occupied much of the life space of Queen Victoria. They were mutually highly dependent and depending, Queen Victoria especially so. When Prince Albert died of typhoid fever, the grief potential was high and Victoria mourned the loss of her consort-cousin intensely, and pathologically, for the rest of her lengthy life. For 35 years she slept beneath a large photograph showing Albert in his coffin, and she had a servant lay out the prince's clothing every morning.

In human relationships there will be some investment of one person in the other, there will be some occupation of each other's life spaces—and the greater the investment the greater the grief potential, the greater the sense of loss when there is a death, the more the loneliness (231). People can be married, they can be parents, they can be close friends, they can be all kinds of things, but it seems inevitable that regardless of the quality of the relationship, if it is close and interdependent, there will be a mutual oc-

cupation of life spaces. That is why the people who share
a marriage relationship with all of its necessary interde-
pendencies will typically be highly invested in each other's
life spaces, and why the impending or actual death of a
spouse is often such a terrifically stressful event, and why
grief in the loss of a marriage partner or emotional spouse
or a child or a close parent tends to be so great. This is
the sort of high grief potential death we need to be concerned about; it is the one that occasions research into the
normal grief syndrome.

> *Death is always and under all*
> *circumstances a tragedy,*
> *for if it is not,*
> *then it means that life itself*
> *has become one.*
> *THEODORE ROOSEVELT*

Engel has pointed out how "The grieving person suddenly
becomes aware of the innumerable ways in which he was
dependent, often quite unconsciously, on the lost person
as a source of gratification and as an essential influence for
his feelings of well-being and effective functioning, his
sense of self" (232). In contradiction, the loss of a parent,
to a child in adult life, is a *relatively* minor event, and it
seems usually to cause a lot less trouble (233, 234). This
seems to be particularly true when the parent is elderly,
especially if he has been separated from the family in some
institution (235). The adult child who has been living with
his parent, who is involved with that person, attached to
and reliant on him, will react more strongly to that parent's
death. Again, it does not seem to be so much a matter of
legal or genetic ties to a person as it is the extent to which
one is involved in the life space of another that determines
the discomfort that will be associated with grief.

65

Aside from grief, two other factors play a part in a widow's reaction to bereavement. These are *stigma* and *deprivation* (236).

Stigma

Parkes believes that stigma is the widow's invisible shroud; she does not want the shroud, but there it is, tainting her, provoking embarrassment and strain in friends, causing female companions to behave as though she has "designs" on their husbands, acting as though they regard her as a threat. One opinion holds that many widows, although perhaps enjoying their independence, are in fact members of a "minority group" and experience many of the problems said to be experienced generally by members of such groups (237).

Deprivation

The reaction to a death will be greatest shortly after the actual loss occurs; but that reaction will decrease in its intensity, Parkes says, and when that happens the reaction to *deprivation* will begin (238).

People who experience a close human relationship, whether it is called shared humanity or love or affectionate mutual regard, will be dependent on one another. That is normal and usual and good. (What is troublesome is the clinging and leech-like overdependency of the markedly insecure.) Dependency takes two forms: to some extent we are dependent on each other to provide closeness, nearness, shared life space, psychological caring and empathy, and regard, but we also depend on each other to perform certain roles and functions in the friendship relationship, the business relationship, or the parenting or the marriage relationships. When one of the people in a relationship dies, both forms of dependency take a beating—there is a psychological vacuum from which we perhaps miss the other person's presence, but there is likely also to be a very practical vacuum, since certain roles and functions are no longer being performed and they need to be performed. Parkes suggests that when a family member dies, one of four things inevitably follows: *1*) necessary roles may not be enacted, *2*) some substitute for the dead member may be sought, *3*) some other family member may have to take over unperformed functions, or *4*) the family unit may fall apart (239, 240). Any of these events may occur, but at least one of them will occur—or all four will occur in some combination.

So the loss of a lover or marriage partner or a close parent can mean many things. It is not just the death itself—complicating losses make the grief more complex, and various things add to it. Parkes says that the widow has lost a husband, but she has also lost all the many other things that the husband may have been or provided (241). Beyond that, his death may be followed by a loss of income which could mean mortgaging or selling the house; perhaps she will have to move to a new neighborhood; her social and economic status may change; and each of these losses may in turn set up its own bereavement (242). The widow may need quickly to learn new roles for her own life, while at the same time she is carrying out old roles with her children who themselves are bereaved (243).

In bereavement a person has the sense of having *lost* some other person, and the loss of that person is difficult, but the things that person provided have also been lost and so there is this second element of bereavement, deprivation. A widow, unlike her primitive ancestor, probably does not have to worry about wild animals at the opening of her cave, but the deceased mate probably provided a great deal more, psychologically and materially, which is now gone. These may be among the reasons that widows of higher education and social class have a greater sense of loss at death, on average, than do those who are less educated and poor, even though they have better resources on which to build their future (244). It may be that these resources, probably exhibited in marriage through independence, lead to the better postbereavement adjustment of women who were relatively independent in the marriage relationship (245).

So, the widow may experience loneliness (246), poverty, lovelessness, sexual frustration, and insecurity, and these deprivations will continue until some new source of supply is found (247). The whole home environment will have changed, and the widow will realize that she is a lone parent (and very likely a lonely one) at a time when, particularly if there has been a long illness, she may be physically and psychologically exhausted (248). A bereaved man for a variety of reasons attributable largely to enculturation, is likely to experience an even more devastating sense of deprivation on the loss of a wife or other emotional partner:

> . . . he may be less flexible or at least less used to concerning himself with matters of children, after-school activities, clothing. This sense of loss may appear as soon as the wife is bedridden or limited in her functioning. There may be a reversal of roles which is more difficult to accept for a man than it is for a woman. Instead of being served, he may be expected to serve, instead of getting some rest after a long day's work, he may watch his wife sit on his couch watching television. Consciously or unconsciously, he may resent these changes, no matter how much he understands the rationale behind it. (249)

Whether or not he expresses it (and he is not likely to), the husband may react to his dying wife as the child responds to a mother's desertion. This is another of the meanings of death in a family summed up by Engel, who commented in 1964 that "the more dependent the relationship, the more difficult will be the task of resolving its loss."

Responses of Children

In something over 5% of American families, children who have not yet reached kindergarten age will experience

the death of a parent or a sibling (250, 251). They must
be allowed freedom to grieve in their own ways; too often,
and for varying reasons, this essential freedom is denied
them.

Various theoreticians, practitioners, and others have been
concerned for years about the extent to which children
grieve, and their arguments have been enthusiastic. (For an
excellent review see Mendelson [252].) Bowlby was of the
opinion in 1960 that an infant type of mourning could be
observed in persons as young as 6 months of age, while in
the same year Anna Freud stated that children who have
not reached the age of "reality testing" are unable to mourn,
and that their grieving experiences are not likely to last
nearly as long as those of the adult; their greatest fear may
be one of abandonment. (The sense of abandonment may
be expected as early as the time when a parent is removed
to a hospital for terminal care. During this time, unless
there are compelling reasons to avoid such interactions,
children should visit the dying parent regularly and maintain contact with that person in whatever appropriate ways
can be managed, and in as nearly a normal way as is possible.) Later, another observer held that children are not
developmentally ready for mourning and that before they
can mourn they must pass through adolescence since this
is the time when most persons learn about giving up love
objects—a sort of mourning initiation (253). Others believe that to a young child, death is no more permanent
than a temporary separation; Anna Freud and also
Burlingham (254) remarked that when a parent dies the
child's behavior is typically appropriate to that person's
having simply gone away, as on a trip, and conversely,
when the parent has actually only gone away, the child
may commonly behave as though the parent had died.
Freud and Burlingham believed that the central point to a
child is simply the parent's presence or absence, and that
ideas as esoteric as actual existence or nonexistence are
beyond the capability of understanding of small youngsters.

Clearly, children do not respond as adults (255); however,
according to Bowlby (256), there are typical stages not un-

like the adult's: protest and disbelief; acceptance, with pain, despair, and disorganization; and hope, as life is re-organized. Similar experiences were observed by McConville, Boag, and Purohit in 1970. It is a mistake for adults to project their feelings onto children and believe from such projections that they know how the children are feeling or, worse, that the children should behave as adults from similar beliefs. At the same time, there is a difference between the reaction to death of an infant and that of an older child (257), and between and among children whose levels of maturation differ (258). The summary situation may have been stated best by Kubler-Ross who believes that children are "the forgotten ones." Reviewing established psychiatric theories of child development, Kubler-Ross has articulated the concepts of death which children possess at differing life stages (259). These range from concerns about separation which are typical of youngsters under 3 years of age; to preoccupation with multilation; to regarding death as something other than permanent by about age 4 or 5; to the "bogey man" or other external intervention which may be important in death ideas of the 5- or 6-year-old. Realistic ideas about dying emerge in the child of perhaps 9 or 10 years of age. (A compelling and moving report of a young child's response to the death of a bird has been provided by Kastenbaum and Aisenberg [260].)

An imperative in helping children is to make certain they receive plenty of love and attention, whether or not they feel compelled to scream for it. It is apparently true that a principal concern of children is who will take care of them, and they must have abundant evidence that they have not been left alone. Family strength and support, particularly at a time of sibling death, are important features in long-term adjustment to death (261).

Levinson has called frankly for families to have pets, since inevitably they will die, and grieving for them gives children the opportunity to rehearse bereavement reactions which they will require in later life (262). Levinson added that *a dead pet should not be replaced immediately*, since to do so gives a false impression to a young child of the permanence of death.

An earlier researcher found that ideas of the meaning of death were common in children of 5 or 6 years of age (263), and others also say that children of this age speak matter-of-factly of death (264); such concepts become more advance by age 7. Logical and biological comprehension was observed at about 8 or 9 years, and the more mature ideas were well established by age 12. Nagy (265) identified three developmental stages in childhood understanding of death: children under 5—unrealistic ideation in relation to sleeping, going on a trip; children 5–9—some acceptance of the finality of death but frequently associated with malevolent personifications, i.e., ghosts, or the "death man," the force of some dead person, or the bogey man (from whom, according to some researchers (266), children believe they can escape by locking the door, hiding under the bed, or running away); children 9 or 10—recognition of death as a universal part of the life cycle.

> Until about the age of four, death for children is a word with little or no meaning; from about five to seven, death is a reversible process; after the age of seven, death begins to be viewed as an irreversible process, caused by a "bad thing"; not until about the age of nine is death viewed as a biological event. (267)

Young children, when angry at their parents, will frequently wish their parents dead, either secretly or perhaps quite openly announcing this wish in a state of anger. The child does not mean dead as adults do, but probably he means to say he wishes the parents would go away, or just "get off my back." When the parent actually does die, or when there is divorce, separation, or desertion, Kubler-Ross cautions that, "Since children cannot yet differentiate between the wish and the deed, they may feel a great deal of remorse and guilt. They will feel responsible for having killed the parents and thus fear a gruesome punishment in retribution" (268). One must remember that the child's previous experience has been that bad things happen to him *when he has misbehaved.*

Kubler-Ross points out, however, that other children may take the separation relatively calmly and utter such statements as "She will come back for the spring vacation," or secretly put an apple out for her—in order to assure that she has enough food for the temporary trip. "If adults, who are upset already during this period, do not understand such children, and reprimand or correct them, the children may hold inside their own way of grieving—which is often a root for later emotional disturbance" (269). Such disturbances may be manifested by deteriorated school performance, physical complaints, withdrawal, depression, and anxiety (270).

Furman has published one incident in which a bereaved widower responded beautifully in what must have been, for him, an awful situation (271): His young daughter reported that the recently dead mother had phoned during the father's absence, to say she would be home for dinner. Apparently the father gave this report a moment's thought, then replied to his daughter, "We both know Mother is not alive any more; maybe sometimes we want to pretend it isn't so because it makes us so unhappy." The response reinforced the reality of death, but showed deep and affectionate understanding of the little girl's feelings.

Behaviors of many children in bereavement are often apparently superficial. These include denial, noise, reversal of affect, boisterousness, regression, short sadness span, apathy, inability to accept death on both intellectual and emotional levels (272), and indifference or a prompt return to playing immediately after learning of some loved person's death. These are often a cover for intense remorseful anxiety and, Nagera believes, for rich fantasy lives in which the dead person seems vitally alive and in an ideal relationship with the child (273).

. . . and after a rather incoherent
interview with my mother, who displayed
a telegram and tried to explain what
"missing" meant, we returned to the
swapping of cigarette cards . . .

DAVID NIVEN
THE MOON'S A BALLOON

A similar fantasy life may affect a child whose sibling
has died and who spends a lot of time talking and playing
with the deceased brother or sister. The phenomenon is
common in both normal and pathological reactions; usually,
if the fantasized sibling remains at the age of the actual person at the time of his death, the survivor will outgrow him.
There is need for professional intervention if the fantasized
companion continues to grow with the survivor (274).
Furman has cautioned that when a child neither masters
nor mourns a childhood bereavement, the effect can remain
alive in his personality (275). Defenses which are alerted
to deal with the attending sadness may then influence his
future ability to make and maintain permanent affectional
relationships, or they may even operate to arrest personality development if the unsatisfactory mourning prohibits
emotional detachment from the lost object. Other contemporary research evidence is available which supports
the idea that children's unresolved grief over the death of a
sibling can lead to detrimental psychological adjustment in
adult life (276).

Furman commented that some very young children will
have a good idea of what death means even while older
children may not, and that a child may seem not to mourn
simply because he does not have the capacity (277).

The potential for possibly strong guilt reactions in children cannot be overstressed. Many children will take on
themselves the blame for a parent's death or for separation
or divorce, imagining that it was something they did or
failed to do which precipitated the event.

Myriad problems beset brothers and sisters of dying children, Gyulay believes (278); these range from jealousy to fear to sensed abandonment and guilt. She actively advocates family therapy to assist with these developments and channel them constructively. Peers and friends may, with every good intention, propose questions which appear "irrelevant, inappropriate, cruel, gruesome or nosy."

Kubler-Ross points out that children are often separated from death situations, perhaps in the belief such situations are "too much" for them. Children may be sent to live with relatives or told that, "Mother has gone for a long trip," or something equally unbelievable. One couple, believing with apparently the best of motives that news of the death of their infant child would be "too much" for a somewhat older sibling, withheld that information from the older child and reported to others that the youngster "didn't know" about the recent death. The child was later observed to be digging holes in his sandbox and burying baby dolls in them (279).

Nagera believes a child who has been told that Daddy has gone to heaven or on a long trip will wonder why Daddy simply doesn't come back (280), and the fantasy of such a return, if encouraged at all, may persist for months and years, perhaps to be "resolved" by the child's decision that "Daddy didn't come back because he didn't like me." The adult who simply admits he doesn't know when confronted by a child's blatant questions is probably doing much better than the well-meaning adult who makes up absurd stories and explanations which would seem faulty to anyone beyond infancy. It is also generally better to discuss death and its implications with children, even very young ones, preferably well in advance of the event when its imminence is known. "If the small child cannot understand fully, nothing is lost; if he understands only a small part, much is gained" (281-285). Phipps has put it this way:

> My observation has been that we are really protecting ourselves from [children's] probing and often brutal questions.

> Because we ourselves are uneasy about our own deaths and about the deaths of others we have set up polite ways of referring to the "departed" to the point of almost denying the reality of death and often, as the result, confusing the grieving process. We as adults have created a conspiracy of silence which denies the children the right to work through their grief. So often adults will comment that a child is obviously "over it," because "he's happy" or "he's playing" or "he never talks about it." Little wonder, since the surviving parent and family give out the message by their pained looks that the children should not ask questions. A child sensitizes himself not to say anything, not to ask, not to emote, not to cry, or to cry along certain prescribed lines. (286)

Kubler-Ross adds that it is not smart to tell a little girl that her brother died because "God loved little boys so much that he took your brother to heaven" (287). She cites the case of one adult woman who got so annoyed with God from just such a confabulation that 30 years later when her son died she sank into a psychotic depression. Other "religious" explanations are not much better. Children think in concrete terms; thus, if heaven is a place where dead people go, then it should be possible to visit there. If God is someone who takes mommies away to the sky, what kind of a guy is God? If Daddy is in some kind of "afterlife," how can he be dead? If Grandma is "asleep," surely she'll wake up. If Sister is only "away on a trip," why wasn't I invited too?

The point is that little of this typical kind of thing is helpful, and it is better to be truthful, with the truth being revealed as best we understand it. The sooner the child can accept the sad reality that has become a part of his young life, the easier his task in dealing with that reality will be.

Researchers have found that the loss of a parent early in life "may be a factor in the later development of a severe depression" (288–293). At least one observer believes that children whose parents have died are profoundly ashamed of this fact (294). Bendiksen studied persons who were ninth graders in 1954, whose families were intact or had previously been altered by death or divorce. His purpose was to assess their adaptation to adult life (295). He found that those whose families had experienced death or divorce had more emotional distress as adults than did the "intact" group, but that there were no important differences among groups in ideas about grief, and that the group from divorce circumstances was significantly more "different" than either the "grief" or "intact" populations. The phenomenon of *both* divorce *and* bereavement was seen as being sociologically important (296).

With regard to adolescence, Kubler-Ross suggests that the time is in itself a difficult one and that the added loss of a parent is too much for some adolescents to endure. (Here we must remember the strongly contradictory feelings which adolescents experience toward their parents. An adolescent going through one of his typical parent-hating cycles is left with an enormous burden of guilt if the parent dies during that inopportune time.) Other observers believe that it is not unusual for adolescents to hypercathect during grieving, to experience and admit fantasies of the parent's return (297–299). This may constitute regression to a child's psychology or a reflection of Kollar's belief that most adolescents refuse to think about death and actively avoid talking about it (300), a finding which is especially interesting when contrasted with Rochlin's report that young children often think about dying and that death is a matter of deep significance to them (301).

Kubler-Ross says that adolescents should be treated like anyone else but perhaps with special care. As with younger children, they should be allowed to ventilate their feelings, whether those feelings be of guilt, anger or plain sadness (302). The suggestion seems especially pertinent when we realize that much of what is believed true of the grief reaction of children and adolescents is the purest supposition, based on nonrandom sampling and observations of emotionally disabled youngsters (303). The absence of solid information concerning the normal reactions of normal children in grief is profound, but we can say for certain that when a child seems to be having a particularly difficult time, psychological referral is desirable. Research evidence is available which suggests that families are reluctant to bring children to professionals for help in mourning, but that the longer the delay, the less successful the treatment (304). Models for therapeutic intervention with children have been proposed by Clark (305) and by Hagin and Corwin (306).

Overlooked Persons

Nurse–clinician Gyulay has called attention to various clusters of persons affected by a death who may or may not be central members of a family which is immediately involved (307). A specialist in the terminal care of leukemic children, Gyulay suggests that in addition to the grief of parents at a time of child death, the strong feelings of others are matters for the concern of persons who would be helpful in a time of bereavement. These include siblings, grandparents, and miscellaneous but "significant others."

Even within the parent diad, Gyulay believes, the father may be overlooked as all sympathetic attention focuses on the mother during a child's terminal illness and at death.

> American society places quite a load on a man's shoulders. From the time he is very young he hears repeatedly, "Be big. Be brave. Be strong." Pain, physical demands, and emotional stresses are endured or deliberately induced to prove his strengths. When he marries, his responsibilities increase. He is never allowed to fail without feeling guilt and shame. With this foundation, he faces tremendous stress when slapped with the reality that his child has a terminal illness. He has usually depended on himself only for strength and emotional solace. Ironically, if he has had a close male confidant—friend or minister—such a person often withdraws because of his own feelings of inadequacies. The responsibility of holding everyone up, but especially himself, is heavy. He may totally deny any emotions.

> Perhaps the most accepted stages of grief allowed fathers are anger or acceptance (because of the "strength" either displays).

Beyond this, the father frequently is not accepted as a partner in providing terminal care, yielding this role to "supermother" and being regarded as "a downright nuisance" whose presence seems regarded as an intrusion. "It seems like the only time they need me is when the damn business office wants me or when the bills come," the father is apt to complain before he withdraws, alone, to be "strong" for fear of breaking down or losing control. Research evidence suggests that those fathers who do least well in grief are those who *feel* alienated from their families during the time of mourning (308). It should be noted that a *feeling* of alienation may be quite distinct from the person's being *actually* pushed aside. What is important here is *how the person is experiencing events*, not necessarily what is actually and objectively going on.

Grandparents, Gyulay believes, are "our biggest problem" in care of terminally ill children; the difficulty arising from the threefold grief of such persons: that for the grandchild, for the child's parent, and for themselves.

> They experience guilt over not recognizing the symptoms and anger that their daughter (or son) did not recognize them. When after all they have offered—advice, financial aid, care, baby sitting, experience, and help—is not accepted, asked for, or is even rejected, they feel guilt, frustration, and anger (309).

"Grandparents are often more alone than any other persons in the grief process," Gyulay argues. "Especially grandfathers—because of their role expectation and triple-layered grief."

Teachers and counselors will be much involved and feeling as events develop and worsen—one research investigation has verified, as might be expected, that teachers' responses to student deaths include the usual pattern of guilt, anger and sadness (310). Another often "forgotten griever" is the child's regular baby sitter. Neighbors, too, grieve and experience their own sorrow.

HELPING THE LIVING

The major focus of these discussions is on those who survive the death of some significant person and on what counselors, allied mental health professionals, and various other persons who happen to be close, can do to help the living in the grief process. Part of the grief syndrome commonly happens before a death occurs, by means of working through what has been called "anticipatory grief" (311, 312), although of course much of the reaction follows. There are some particularly helpful activities which the helper needs to keep in mind as necessary prebereavement concerns; these have to do with the desirability of his being available to family and friends, or helping them in their preparation for the death of their loved person, in coping with their own defenses, in encouraging and allowing ventilation of considerable affect—and strategies for putting all of these things together in a helpful scheme. According to Fulton and Fulton, the family and close friends may actually display little emotion or even none at all, if the death has been anticipated and if grief has already been worked through (313).

Research investigations reported independently by Ball (314) and by Vachon (315) suggest that young widows, in particular, take bereavement more comfortably when it has been anticipated, than when its occurrence has been sudden.

Availability

Elisabeth Kubler-Ross has given primary attention to problems of the dying, but she hasn't forgotten the family. She refers to

. . . the time when the relatives walk up and down the hospital hallways, tormented by the waiting, not knowing if they should leave to attend the living or stay to be around for the moment of death. This is the time when it is too late for words, and yet the time when the relatives cry the loudest for help—with or without words. It is too late for medical intervention . . . but it is also too early for a final separation from the dying. It is the hardest time for the next of kin as he either wishes to take off, to get it over with; or he desperately clings to something that he is in the process of losing forever. It is the time for the therapy of silence with the patient and availability for the relatives (316).

An example of extraordinary sensitivity and helpfulness has been provided by nurse–clinician Gyulay:

One of the most beautiful examples of ministry I have ever seen is that of a young white pastor of a black family, whose seven-year-old leukemic boy, Andy, was dying of intracranial bleeding. He stayed all day quietly in the background. He helped the nurses change the bed, a constant activity due to incontinency. He rarely said anything. Periodically, he would go out and come back quickly with cups of hot coffee. When the parents requested it, he would gather them around the bed and pray. The periods of silence and of quiet crying were unexplainably comfortable under such circumstances. When he left the room for coffee, the mother stated, "You know, he does this with every family who needs him. He's always there—quiet, caring, and loving." (317)

Engel suggests that the helper

. . . will require patience, tact, and warm sympathy for the person who refuses to acknowledge the truth of the news as well as for the person who literally collapses or loses control. Understanding that these are the ways that people have to protect themselves from the overwhelming should provide [the helper] with the confidence that patient, gentle, and feeling reiteration of the reality coupled with the personal demonstration of a wish to help will go far in helping the grief-stricken over this difficult strait. Most important is encouraging the bereaved person to cry. (318)

Preparation

Usually, there is a time of preparation which comes before the last lonely moments. The preparatory period may be one of months, it may be a much shorter time, or there may be—as in cases of sudden, accidental death—no preparation time at all. Although "one is truly never prepared for the reality of death and its permanence" (319), normally there is at least some time for the family to get things together as best they are able—there will be a waiting time, a time of the death watch.

According to Parkes the most common way of mitigating the pain of grieving is not to believe the loss is imminent or has occurred (320). Virtually all bereaved people will say in one form or another, "I can't believe it's true," and such expressions are likely as long as a year after the death. "It's like a dream; I'll wake up and it'll be all right"; "This is a nightmare, someone tell me it's only a nightmare." Disbelief is as common before death as it is after. It is common for persons who have been advised that death in the immediate future is inevitable to deny the accuracy of that report; they either doubt the diagnosis, or they accept it and believe that the illness is not as serious as the physicians believe. They will often rage at the medical staff or seek other opinions, but at the same time they will inform family and friends and make essential plans. The helper should bear in mind, though, that sometimes a psychological curse lurks nearby. The "Lazarus Syndrome" refers to the situation in which close persons have made full emotional adjustment to an imminent death which does not happen when it is supposed to—the dying person has lived through the crisis. His survivors, having accommodated to the anticipated death, are left in emotional isolation from the supposedly dying person, commonly with a heavy load of

guilt for having "wished him dead." Lazarus can be anticipated any time someone has weathered a supposedly terminal medical emergency. Beyond that, excessive hostility
toward the medical staff during the middle stages of a final
illness may serve as an indicator that mothers of dying children are maintaining denial and a warning that they may
have particularly difficult problems at the death (321).
Persons who employ denial throughout the term of any in-
curable illness are likely to respond psychologically to the
actual death as persons typically do to deaths which are
sudden and unexpected (322, 323).

Relatively young widows and widowers demonstrate
more profound grief reactions in losses which are sudden,
and the disturbance can continue for a full year (324–329).
It is not clear how important preparation time is in alleviat-
ing the discomfort of grief, but it seems that time to prepare oneself for the likelihood of bereavement does have
at least some effect on the later reaction. Acute grief reactions in response to sudden deaths are characterized by
fear, guilt, denial, anger (330) and abnormal defensive activities and hallucinations (331), with only vague recall for
the period immediately following death (332). These responses are not unlike those observed in other grief reactions, but they seem to be more pronounced when death is
unexpected. Clayton (332) has denied that one can predict
the severity of a bereavement reaction on the basis of time
available for anticipatory grief work (333); but this particular study has been criticized by Parkes who pointed out that
the average age of widows in the Clayton study was 61, an
age at which disengagement may have already begun. Parkes
continues to insist that time to prepare is particularly important for the relatively young (334). Skelton and
Dominian found that reactions to the deaths of husbands
were more severe among women under 45 than among
women beyond that age (335).

But again, even anticipatory knowledge may not help
grieving persons if they suppress anticipatory grief for fear
of upsetting the dying person. Kubler-Ross says, "An un-

derstanding helper can contribute a lot in helping [members of the family and close friends] to maintain a sound balance between serving the patient and respecting their own needs," but she adds that "family members should handle their energies economically and not exert themselves to a point that they collapse when they are most needed" (336).

Defenses

Parkes tells us that while they are waiting for a death to occur, family and friends will tend to minimize the seriousness of events and they will minimize the gravity of the ill person's condition as they relate to friends, family, business associates. In fact, as was mentioned before, there is a tendency to minimize the seriousness of the patient's condition in interactions with the dying person himself (337). There is likely to be unreasonable optimism and continued hope for recovery long after many of the medical people have given up and withdrawn.

In this connection, counselors and other helpers ought to know well in advance that in a time of terminal illness they should not expect physicians to provide much help for the family. They will keep the family waiting (according to Mauksch, that is one strategy some medical persons use to gain power (338); one virtually always waits past the established time for an appointment, and this reinforces the supplicant–provider relationship). But when a physician finally appears in the hospital during a terminal illness to offer assistance it is an added bonus and normally a helpful and comforting one. However, the reality is that once events are in their final stages, the physician will do what he can to make things as comfortable as possible for the dying person, and he will leave appropriate medication orders for the nurses to follow, in their often too–sterile routine, but he probably will not spend much time with the family. As Gyulay put it (339): "Physicians make their rounds (which often become shorter and less frequent as death nears) and frequently they have responsibilities elsewhere." The worse things get, the less frequently the physician is likely to be present (340). He may be long on science, but he is apt to be short on art (341). He may very well displace his anger by attacking the nursing staff (342). There are reasons for this.

First, we have to understand something of the physician's psychology. One would not expect it, perhaps, but death makes many physicians acutely uncomfortable—they have trouble dealing with it. They may see the dying patient as a threat (343). Indeed, the whole scientific process of studying the psychology of gravely ill and dying persons has been hampered by physicians who have flatly refused to permit interviews with such persons, when the interviews could have done no conceivable harm and yielded only information which might have been useful. (These problems have been discussed by Kubler-Ross [344] and by Mauksch [345], especially on page 15.) In a 1969 study, Schoenberg found that many student nurses become intensely anxious when confronted with death and that a typical response is one of emotional withdrawal, avoidance, and isolation. Mervyn, a nurse who holds a counseling master's degree (346), asks, "How many nurses or physicians can be comfortable in the presence of someone whose dying forecasts their own future?"

But beyond this particular difficulty (which, after all, confronts everyone), the physician's orientation is toward keeping people alive, and while he knows that no one lives forever and recognizes with the 17th Century's Thomas Browne that "death is the cure of all diseases," he is still likely to experience any patient death as a personal defeat. None of us, especially physicians, likes to go among strangers and admit we have lost, confess we are less than omnipotent, and then talk about it. We are particularly not apt to volunteer for such missions when we can guess from experience that at least some people in the situation will hold us personally responsible for events and become angry with us. Mauksch tells us that "Somewhere within the hospital culture lurks the awesome expectation that, while all other human beings are permitted to make mistakes and to commit errors, physicians and nurses must not" (347). Buying into this role expectations, many physicians who are in fact acutely moved and possessed of extraordinarily strong affect at a time of patient death may simply not be able to allow themselves freedom to ventilate those strong feelings.

The physician may not even say that the patient is dying, but refer instead to an array of obviously morbid symptoms which anyone would recognize as deadly. Some physicians will not even say the word "fatal." Some will not return phone calls from members of the family. It is interesting, too, to note that no one dies in a hospital—one "expires," or one is "lost on the table," to quote an observation admitting of appalling carelessness which may be made by hospital workers. But, lest we be too quick to condemn hospital staffs for playing semantic denial games, let's notice that few people die elsewhere. Edgar didn't die, thank God, Edgar "passed away," or Edgar "met his Maker," or Edgar "didn't make it," or Edgar "was taken." A pity. Edgar would have been better off dead.

Binger and his colleagues explained it this way, as an observation related to their investigation of the emotional impact of child deaths from leukemia:

> The (physician) is distressed and often feels guilty about the failure of therapy. Simultaneously he is troubled by his own fears and anxieties about death and feels inadequate to support the dying child and his parents. Faced with these conflicts he often avoids the patient or family or makes himself unapproachable by presenting a facade of busyness, impatience, or formality. Thus, at a time when most needed, the professional often assumes a neutral or even negative role in contacts with the family of the dying. (348)

So the helper is well advised to realize that in a death situation his best ally, and the best ally of the family, is far more likely to be the nurse than the attending physician. This is the one person who is close to the dying person throughout his terminal illness, who sees him regularly, who helps in a variety of ways, and who is the medical person most likely to be with him when he dies—unless the nurse, too, is well protected behind a defensive shield of callousness (which would be understandable if not particularly helpful), or preoccupied with the grief *she* can experience when a patient dies. Fulton reported that many nurses perceive themselves to be far more upset at many deaths than are members of the families (349); Natterson and Knudson reported in one study that subsequent to infant deaths, hospital personnel become depressive, guilty, and self-examining (350); whoever cares for the person in the last stages of his terminal illness may experience a sense of worthlessness and of "nothing more to live for" after the death—a profound sense of emptiness, according to Calkins (351); and Gyulay points out that nurses in high mortality specialties are in a psychological state of chronic grief (352-354). It is often true, though, that nurses can be hidden behind defenses (overconcern with composure, busyness with tasks, efficiency, avoidance) which are designed to keep them from emotional hurt at a time of death (355, 356) or simply swamped by work. Mervyn (357) discussed this problem in 1971:

> I remember vividly my own feelings as a head nurse on a short-staffed 3 p.m. to 11 p.m. shift when a middle-aged patient suffered a myocardial infarction at 10 p.m. The organizational details were time-consuming. The bedside oxygen outlet was not functioning, and a portable oxygen tank had to be obtained. My one assistant, a nurse's aid, was behind schedule, so a "float" nurse had to be called. The patient's physician could not be located. I was concerned that the patient's relatives would arrive before the physician, and I then would be faced with circumventing their questions because this physician did not allow nurses to explain impending or actual deaths. As a result of all this, unit work was thoroughly disrupted. When the night

shift came on duty, I was one hour behind schedule; medications still to be given, much charting still to be done, and, afterward, a detailed explanation to be written for overtime—in duplicate. In the myriad organization details with which I contended, emotionally supportive nursing was lost. (358–362)

Yet another institutional person who may be involved emotionally in a death, even while seemingly remote from the situation, is the hospital pharmacist. This person is able to follow the progress of a final illness by means of medicines which are being ordered, and is often upset, if only briefly so, when he notices that the orders have stopped coming.

The problem of accepting death is not limited to hospitals. Routine and ritual are present in nursing homes too, where personnel may see their mission as one of caring for chronically ill persons rather than for those who are terminally ill, and where patient deaths are distressing to staff and patients. Depending on the situation and the particular nursing home, staff personnel may be hostile and critical toward the family, particularly when family visits are infrequent and the patient relies on staff members for the social and personal support normally provided by a family (363).

Dying people go through a phase in which they try to bargain for more time, for renewed time. Family and friends can do the same thing. Those who imagine, under the impact of some temporary or habitual delusional system, that their thought processes can influence events which are beyond human control may very well make implorations via prayer or direct confrontation with the medical staff, which asks that they be "taken" instead, or in which they propose to "be good" if only the doomed life can be saved, or in which they promise to go to church faithfully, or build a new wing for the hospital. Intentions here are impeccable but the behaviors are still a kind of defense which suggests that the trauma everyone is experiencing constitutes some kind of punishment for bad behavior, and that if the family member or friend will only straighten up and conduct himself properly the bad things that are happening will go away.

Ventilation

Members of the family and close friends will have anger, and with it they will have a need to ventilate. Kubler-Ross tells us that the family will be angry with the physician and hospital staff and that much guilt will be in evidence (364). She believes that family members often feel a need to blame themselves for the fatal illness or to assume a (usually) unwarranted burden of guilt for not doing more than they did to correct the situation (365). According to Engel (365), this causes the massive projection of guilt against everyone in the environment which is so often seen when a death is imminent. It is either a projection of guilt or a reaction to circumstances about which complaints are actually justified. (Funeral directors observe that again and again bereaved people will compulsively tell them in great detail about the course of a final illness—some refer to this as a purging.)

The problem of guilt in grief reactions is a profound one, and it comes up again and again. Somehow bereaved people experience and express all kinds of guilt about their own presumed negligence in taking care of the sick person (including, perhaps, their memory of annoyance when the dying person was irritable, critical, or demanding and their sense of relief at the death) (367). More often the guilt relates to their own perceived inadequacies in relating successfully to the dying person in his lifetime, to important things which were left unsaid or undone—and these kinds of guilt give survivors considerable difficulty. More will be said about this later, but guilt as part of the grief reaction has not been studied thoroughly yet. It will be in time, and the results will be brought together. Meanwhile, counselors

and other helpers should be prepared to expect guilt expressions from members of the family while a death is happening and afterward.

Sometimes the guilt is deserved. Perhaps the surviving
family member was incautious, unobservant, or careless,
but so far there is no evidence of the influence of deserved
guilt on a grief reaction vis-a-vis undeserved guilt, which
seems always to be present and always to be painful, even
when it relates only to the oversights of usual human interactions with people we expect to be around forever.
Kubler-Ross says that people who are having this kind of
guilt can be reassured, but she suggests that the reassurance
may constitute nothing more than supportive social chit-
chat and that that probably is not enough. Usually there is
a reason behind the guilt, Kubler-Ross believes. Very possibly there are feelings of anger toward the dying person
which are difficult to articulate for the obvious reason that
it is socially awkward and psychologically painful to ventilate anger toward someone who is dying.

As Samuel Butler commented in the 19th Century, "It
costs a lot of money to die comfortably." It still does. An
important aspect of the guilt problem is the matter of financing a death (or for that matter a life) in a hospital.
The United States is the only nation in the civilized world
which does not, at this writing, have a social scheme for de-
livering basic physical health care services to its citizens, and
in which enormous profits are allowed those few who de-
liver such services and who insure their delivery. These
costs can be both devastating and catastrophic to families
below the upper income level, even when they have "better"
insurance programs. Most persons simply lack financial resources to pay for the dying of a family member, and occasionally, at least, their thoughts must turn to this in-
credible but very real difficulty. The fact that they are
thinking of money (as they must) while a loved and close
person is mortally ill cannot help but make its contribution
to the guilt reaction.

Still, if family members can express and work through their anger, preferably in privacy with some helper, this may be enough to alleviate the feelings of guilt (368). The opportunity to do so may in fact be one of the most useful contributions the helper can make during a death watch. Parkes observes that persons who experience the greatest deterioration in health following bereavement are the ones who have not been permitted by those around them to talk about the death or to express their feelings openly (369). Kubler-Ross agrees, saying, "A high percentage of widowers and widows seen in clinics and by private physicians present themselves with somatic symptoms as a result of the failure to work through their grief and guilt" (370). The wife of a terminally ill patient will probably have resentment, and this is to be expected, particularly if family, neighbors and friends are not supportive. However, "an understanding neighbor who does not come to 'hear the latest' but who comes to relieve the mother of some of her tasks, cook, or take the children to a play can be greatly appreciated" (371).

Ventilation includes the fears of family and friends. These fears of the patient's pain, of one's own possible loss of control and inability to cope, of isolation and loneliness, of being unable to love again, of finality (372) are among those which must be expressed when need is present and are among those to which an empathic helper will be sensitive. Gyulay also argues that relatives and others must be informed fully of potentially frightening environmental equipment and activities which may be new to their experience: breathing changes, seizures, spiking fevers, drainage, incontinence, and bleeding. The sounds and workings of the respirator, catheter, oxygen gauge, humidifier, pump, heart monitor, and the like, may be ominous to those who are unfamiliar with health care environments. An oscilloscope which accidentally becomes unplugged may, to the medical personnel, be simply an unplugged oscilloscope; to family and friends, it may be stimulus for panic.

Departure

The patient's effort to separate himself gradually from persons who have been close to him is often misinterpreted by the immediate family as rejection. Kubler-Ross suggests that such families be told that only the dying patient who has been able to find a peaceful acceptance of his dying is able to withdraw in this way, and that this fact might represent a cause for comfort and solace to the family rather than an excuse for resentment. This is the time when the family needs the most support and the patient needs the least although this does not mean the patient should be abandoned. "A patient who has reached this stage of acceptance and decathexis usually requires little in terms of interpersonal relationship. If the meaning of this detachment is not explained to the family, problems can arise" (373).

Counselors, psychologists, or other psychotherapeutic professionals probably will not be immediately at hand when death comes, but other professionals may be—the nurses, almost certainly; perhaps the clergy (374–378). Engel speaks directly to nurses and clergy when he says:

> The request to see and take leave of the dying or dead patient should not be denied on the ground that it may be too upsetting or that it will disturb the floor routine. This need to take leave, to ask forgiveness, to touch, kiss, or caress the dying or dead loved one, to take a lock of hair, is of overwhelming importance to some and will not be requested by those for whom it will be disturbing. (379)

Let them say goodbye.

PSYCHOLOGICAL PHASES OF GRIEF

Survivors will react to a death even when the death has been a long time in coming or when it follows a period of many months in which someone has been functionally dead (380) and in which much anticipatory grief work has been done. The strength of the reaction will vary among individuals although the timeliness or untimeliness of a death seems to affect the magnitude of a grief reaction and determines to some extent whether it is of high or low grief potential. According to Parkes there is a big difference between the quiet slipping away of an old man whose death is anticipated (and has been, perhaps, for years) and that of some young person in his prime (381).

> *There is a great difference between*
> *going off in warm blood like Romeo,*
> *and making one's exit like a frog*
> *in a frost.*
>
> *KEATS*
> *PERSONAL CORRESPONDENCE*

According to Levinson the more severe grief reaction which follows a sudden and unexpected death results from the survivor's lack of opportunity to fully preceive what has happened, to give up the dead person, and to make restitution (382). Where death is not unexpected, as after a long illness or when the person is elderly, it is generally accepted that a period in which to adjust to the death will make the actual bereavement easier and perhaps shorter. The preparatory period allows survivors to work through denial, anger, and guilt concerning the impending death, to accept its inevitability, and gradually to return to activities not involving the dying person (383, 384). Those who complete this anticipatory grieving will tend to withdraw from the dying person and will perhaps feel relatively little emotion and possibly even relief at the actual death (384, 385). They may actually have little need for or interest in the funeral rituals or grief processing at the time of death (386–390).

Regardless of what kind of death we are concerned with, the survivors will go through stages of grief although they may find them hard at the time to describe (391). We can study these phases of grief and become familiar with them without losing sight of Mendelson's precautionary note about "the deadening effect of trying to squeeze human reactions too narrowly into arbitrarily delimited definitions" (392), or Lopata's (1975) assertion that widows, in particular, may sense pressure to "go through the stages" and may feel rejected when they cannot (393). A map of unexplored territory can be helpful, but we must remember it is only a map and no territory is ever fully explored.

In 1953, after studying separation behaviors among children aged 1 to 4 years, Robertson called the stages *protest*, *despair*, and *detachment*. Later, Bowlby (394) wrote that the grieving person's thoughts and behaviors will be directed toward the lost object, he will exhibit anger, he will appeal for help and show despair, and ultimately he will direct his affection toward some new love object—an acceptance of the protest–despair–detachment concept (395). Moss and Moss describe a sequence in the grief process involving movement from denial to acceptance, from shocked bewilderment to understanding awareness, from guilt and self-blame to exoneration and restitution (396). Numbness will merge into pining, and pining into depression, and only after this necessary depression will recovery begin (397). Since transition from one stage to another is not always clear-cut and precise, a variety of pictures may emerge over the grieving period, with oscillation being common among the phases (398). It is this fact which can set up a particularly troublesome situation, however. When parents are grieving the death of a child, or when more than one person is involved in a bereavement reaction, the persons may experience various elements of the grief reaction at different times and thus be out of phase or dyssynchronous with each other. This requires that such parties maintain open communication and patience with each other. This is one of the reasons, among several which could probably be cited, why the generalization can be made that whenever a child dies, the parents and surviving children should have at least a couple of consultations with some professional mental health worker.

Parkes has suggested that there are seven principal components of grief (399), most of which will occur in any reaction to bereavement—not necessarily in this order, because he believes that the stages overlap and that elements of various phases will occur and recur at varying times through the period of bereavement.

He says there will be a *process of realization* in which the bereaved person moves from denial or avoidance of recognition of the loss toward its acceptance. There will also be an *alarm* reaction, a time of restlessness, anxiety, and the various physiological accompaniments of fear. Third, Parkes suggests that the bereaved individual will experience an *urge to search* for the dead person, to try to find that person in some form. Further, there will be *anger and guilt*—the anger will go in all sorts of outward directions, but the guilt will be directed inward. The bereaved person will experience feelings of internal loss, of mutilation, in reaction to that part of his life space which has suddenly disappeared. There may be what Parkes calls an "identification phenomenon," in which the bereaved person adopts the traits, mannerisms, or even the lethal symptoms of the dead person, and during which the bereaved person may experience his deceased friend as being inside himself. Parkes tells us that there are some pathologic variants of the usual grief pattern. These will be explored in more detail later on, but in sum they involve excessive reactions and prolonged or inhibited reactions which may emerge in distorted form.

Against this array of grief stages, we have Kubler-Ross suggesting that bereaved persons go through pretty much the same stages as do the dying: denial and isolation, anger, bargaining, depression, and acceptance (400). Since Kubler-Ross wrote *On Death and Dying* before Parkes came out with his *Studies of Grief in Adult Life*, and since there is no citation of the Kubler-Ross observations in Parkes' bibliography, we have to assume that the two were unfamiliar with each other's major works at the time of their primary efforts (although Kubler-Ross cites a couple of the early Parkes journal articles). It seem legitimate to take the findings of these two principal researchers/observers and from their work, supplemented by that of various others, put together what we can call the psychological stages of bereavement. In doing this we obviously rely more heavily on Parkes than on Kubler-Ross, since it was Parkes who gave his principal attention to the bereaved whereas Kubler-Ross focused primary attention on the dying.

The phases of bereavement tend to follow the order in which we consider them here, but they also seem to recur from time to time. In bereavement reactions we are not always contending with a consecutive series of stages through which an individual progresses, because any of the components can show up, in varying levels of strength, at differing times during the grieving process. The phases tend to be strongest in the order given, always with a precipitating event and nearly always with some form of acceptance, since grief is usually self-limiting.

We can call the psychological stages of bereavement *denial, separation anxiety, anger and guilt, depression,* and *acceptance.*

Denial

The first reaction to news that some loved person is about to die or that some such person has died suddenly is one of protest. Denial and resistance constitute the principal psychological features (401, 402). The truth of the matter is something that is extraordinarily painful to accept, and so for a time we do not accept it. Engel said, "The grieving person attempts to refute, to deny, to dispute the reality of the event; he may throw himself on the body to find some sign of life" (403). Parkes tells us that the moment of death is likely to be followed by a feeling of numbness or of blunting, which may come on immediately but certainly within a few minutes (404). The numbness and blunting may last for a few hours or even a few days, and some form of denial may on occasion last for months (405, 406). Falek and Britton have suggested that a characteristic of denial is its effect of preventing a person from initiating any behavioral change of a kind which might be helpful at a time of bereavement (407). The person who is responding to sudden marital or other social separation with a grief reaction may have a more difficult time with the unconscious denial process than will someone who is responding to a death. When the "lost" person is still living, some hope may remain in the deserted person's mind that the relationship can be repaired, and this fact may delay resolution of the bereavement far longer than would be desirable.

During this time of denial the reality of events may not register, or there may be disbelief or expression of an idea that some mistake has been made. There may be rigid unresponsiveness or a condition of dazed emotional shut-down and numb indifference (408). Homeostasis will be out of kilter (409); the family may even refuse permission for autopsy. The reality of events may not be brought home until the funeral and interment, and even then there are rare occasions when a widow must be restrained from trying to rescue her husband from the coffin as it's being lowered into the.ground. In some cases, elements of the denial defense may persist for months. Barinbaum (410), in conducting group counseling sessions with mothers and widows of the Yom Kippur War, found that denial was an important feature in early therapeutic reactions, even well after the war had ended. Professional literature contains a report of a 65-year-old woman who wrote letters for 6 months to her dead husband (411), and there are reports of bereaved persons who have kept bodies around the house from a week to 10 years (412).

Denial may in part be psychological and in part socially conditioned by circumstances and environment. Funeral homes contribute in at least some measure to the denial process. Hearses are not "hearses," they are "coaches" or "professional cars." Flowers are not flowers, they are "floral tributes." Corpses are "loved ones." The dead person's remains are on view in a "slumber room" (413).

The numbness and blunting are typically transient, and they are rarely severe. The immediate reaction is one of denial, particularly when the news is unexpected. The friend or wife may say "No!" or "It can't be true." Again, the psychological mechanism is, if we say a thing isn't true, it isn't; even as adults we sometimes have to get fantasy and reality mixed up in order to defend ourselves. We have to keep truth away by shouting "No!" at it.

So that is what a relative or friend may say when he first gets news of a terminal illness or sudden death if there has been no preparatory time. Denial. There will be the numb shock, the "numbed feeling in which the grief-stricken person does not permit himself any thoughts or feelings which acknowledge the reality of the death" (414). There may be momentary speechlessness, perhaps a blank look, a dazed inability to move, perhaps grossly disturbed behaviors; the person may even collapse on the floor and beat his head. He has taken a terrific psychological blow, and his response may be very much like the psychological response to trauma: shock, and with it the vacant look with dilated pupils; shallow, fast, irregular anxious breathing; fast but weak pulse; cool and clammy skin with perspiration; perhaps nausea; a lot of restlessness; marked thirst is likely to be noticed. The person may seem "out of contact and it may be difficult to gain his attention" (415). The shock reaction will probably pass fairly quickly (although according to Engel the reaction can last up to several hours or even days), but it can be anticipated. On occasion people faint, so it is a good idea when one is about to present really bad news to have the person seated—first, to keep him from hurting himself if in fact he does fall, but also because if one asks the person to sit, he may recognize through the social convention of being asked to sit that he is being prepared for very bad news.

Parkes says that bereavement evokes arousal and with it the alarm reaction (416). He points out that the grieving person is in a state of high arousal much of the time, and sometimes this arousal approaches panic (417). The person is likely to tremble a lot and will report that his "nerves are on edge." He will have feelings of fright, perhaps of panic. When any animal is in a state of alarm, its physiological system will alter to support fight or flight and to set aside functions of less immediate importance. For these reasons the alarmed person will have an elevated rate of heart activity, there will be an increase in respiration and muscular tension, better vision, sweating, and higher levels of energy. (Knowing that bereaved persons, in comparison to the non-bereaved, have a higher mortality rate from coronary thrombosis during the year after bereavement, and particularly during the first 6 months, counselors and other professionals may grow concerned when a grieving person complains of palpitations and feelings of fullness in the chest. These feelings are normal in anxiety, they are normal in grief, and they do not suggest that the bereaved person is about to have a heart attack unless the helper is also hearing about and observing other symptoms which could suggest that possibility.)

At the same time, digestive and other functions of lower survival priority will be inhibited, so that the alarmed person is likely to have a dry mouth because his saliva has slowed down markedly. The person is in a state of readiness for instant action. One who remains in a state of stressful response to alarm for more than a short period of time will then experience strain (418).

We can all tolerate strain, but the threshold differs among persons. Some cannot take much. Parkes says that when the strain is too great, the person will be unable to cope and will be overwhelmed by circumstances. He may persevere in inappropriate behaviors, or he may behave in a disorganized, fragmented way. When a grieving person is clinging to old ideas which no longer apply, it can be assumed, according to Parkes, that the person has experienced intolerable strain—he is not able to contend with present difficulties so instead of fighting he flees (419).

Parkes tells us that the physiological reactions to alarm include loss of appetite (and subsequently of weight), digestive distress, palpitations, and various other aches and pains (420). Insomnia is so often present in some measure, often in severe form, that its presence can be regarded as a classic symptom—and even when the person gets to sleep, he may awaken more frequently than has been typical for him. During the first few weeks of bereavement the grieving person is likely to be uninterested in food, and mouth dryness will be evident; he may complain that the whole thing has "hit the pit of his stomach." Headaches are usually seen as relating to tension or "pressure in the head." Persons will describe themselves as jumpy and irritable. There is an overall restless anxiety.

> *Grief is proud,*
> *And makes his owner stoop.*
> *SHAKESPEARE*
> *KING JOHN*

Anyone who brings unwelcome information is resisted—that is why family and friends are often hostile toward physicians and hospital staff (the family can be like those kings who used to execute messengers who brought bad news); but the same resistance may be exhibited toward anyone who comes around to offer consolation, and one may as well expect it. Consoling people are evidence that a terrible situation is real, and such persons may be resisted. Maybe this is why we tend not to use the word "dead" when we are around the bereaved and why we behave as though the dead were really only sleeping.

While traditional Judaism forces mourners to face the reality of death and to do so promptly and efficiently (421), Parkes reports that the Episcopal funeral service mentions "rest" three times and insists on 13 separate occasions that the person is awaiting resurrection (422). Both of these Christian ideas deny what is really happening, and contribute to the fantasy that a death is not a death. The word "dead" does not appear at all in the Episcopal funeral service—and religious services for children sometimes address themselves to the "roses in God's garden," which seems to be beside the point of a youngster's dying. Gyulay (423) believes that many pastors become anxious at the time of death and fall back on such trite formulas as "He'll be an angel in heaven," or "It's God's will" (424–427). These sterile pronouncements are doubtlessly well meant, but they make the clergyman less a minister than an apologist for God's brutalities. Gyulay says that "if a family is told often that 'this is God's will' by a man of God, they fear expressing what they really feel and experience guilt over these 'wrong' feelings (423)." Apparently, quite different responses can be associated with other cultures, Samoa being an example (428).

It should be noted that any persistent denial of the reality of a death, an exaggeration or prolongation of the normal response, particularly when affected persons behave as though the deceased were still alive and the general affect is happy or otherwise normal, should indicate referral to a psychologist or psychiatrist (429, 430).

Separation Anxiety

According to Parkes, the clinical diagnosis most often suggested for grief reaction is "reactive depression," but he believes the more appropriate diagnostic lable is "separation anxiety" (431). This is an idea associated with Rank's beliefs regarding infants who have been separated from their mothers, but in this case translated to adults who revert psychologically for a time to an infantile state (432). The classic symptoms of anxiety include apathy, hyperactivity, refusal of food, and sleeplessness. Pining, yearning, and searching are all part of the picture as it emerges in grief.

Each of these behaviors is consistent with the Falek and Britton idea (433) that anxiety results when persons respond to stress by recognizing, after initial denial, that something needs to be done and *begin to behave*—even, apparently, inappropriately and anxiously.

Pining and Yearning. Prominent features of separation anxiety are pining and yearning, with searching coming later, and that is the characteristic clinical picture in grief: an anguished awareness of the reality which develops in minutes or perhaps in hours (434), constituting what Prado de Molina (435) has called "external acceptance," followed by pining and yearning, particularly after the first couple of days (436).

> Within a short time the reality of the death and its meaning as a loss begins more and more to penetrate consciousness in the form of an acute and increasing awareness of the pain and anguish of the loss, the feeling of something missing or lost, often felt as a painful emptiness in the chest or epigastrium. The effect experienced is primarily acute sadness, with which may be admixed some anxiety, helplessness or hopelessness. The environment seems frustrating and empty since it no longer includes the loved person. (437)

Parkes describes it in some detail, identifying as important the strong attachment which young children have to their mothers and, in time, to other persons who take on protective and nurturant properties of the home (438). Separation, either temporary or permanent, causes us to behave as we did in infancy when we behaved in a way which we had learned would result in the return of mother, and that is the memory and the resultant behavior which recurs during the yearning phase (439).

Engel said, "The grieving person . . . sends out various behavioral cries for help, to which his fellow men respond. Failure or inability to emit the cry or to elicit a response are fraught with dire implications for recovery" (440).

And so, the natural need, during pining and yearning, is to *cry*, often *an overpowering urge to cry* during the grieving process, during reaction to any loss or suffering, a need to express helplessness, to gain needed sympathy and help, a learned behavior which is now enacted *from an unconscious level* to attract and secure prompt comfort in the form of mother (441).

Crying and Sobbing. Anguished displays are not unusual at this time.

> It is during this period that the greatest degree of anguish or despair, within the limits imposed by cultural patterns, is experienced and expressed. Some cultures demand loud and public lamentation, whereas others expect restraint. Familiarity with such cultural patterns is necessary in evaluating the appropriateness of a grief response. Regardless of such factors, the wish and need to cry is strong, and crying seems to fulfill an important function in the work of (grieving). (442)

Engel believes that

> in general, crying seems to involve both an acknowledgement of the loss and the regression to a more helpless and childlike status. In the latter sense, crying is a communication. The grief-stricken person who cries is the recipient of certain kinds of support and help from the group, although this varies greatly in different cultures. Grief is one situation in which the tears of an adult are generally accepted and understood and the person who is able to cry still feels self-respect and worthfulness and that he is deserving of help. (443)

The grieving person may "accept a more dependent relation with family members and old friends" (444), and this dependency is understood and accepted; friends seem to support each other and to assist the family. It helps. Hansel had Gretel, and Gretel had Hansel, and that must have offered comfort as they wandered their bewitched, dark woods.

Parkes reminds us (445) that Darwin believed human sobbing was a kind of muted weeping—the cry itself is stifled, but the spasmodic movements of preparatory deep breathing remain. (One can see these inspirations, appropriate to a person who is about to shout, in any youngster just before or just after he cries.) The sobbing is a semi-controlled shouting for the lost person. Observe someone in grief and a typical facial expression will be seen which seems to be a struggle between the overpowering need to shout or cry, and equally powerful *felt* social demands to exhibit strength and to suppress such "childish" behaviors as wailing from despair; thus, the battle: the raised inner eyebrows, the wrinkled forehead, the contracted facial muscles. The sighs which one also hears from grieving persons are inhibited spasms of crying or sobbing—one is "choked with grief," one experiences "a painful emptiness in the chest" (446).

Psychologist E. Charles Welsh tells grieving clients, "Don't shut off your tears—they're part of the price of your love." But Engel cautioned that not everyone cries (447). Some people do not feel the need. To them the death has perhaps been one of what Fulton and Fulton call low grief potential (448); others inhibit the response because of environmental or cultural demands and do their crying alone or inwardly; still others want to cry but cannot—instead, perhaps, they exhibit rigid unresponsiveness. It is this last response to the crying impulse—inability to cry—which is more serious. "It is most likely to occur when the relationship with the dead person [was] highly ambivalent and when the survivor is experiencing a good deal of guilt and shame" (449).

In the presence of such denial mechanisms the work of mourning does not take place or takes place incompletely. A psychotic depression, manic reaction or some other illness, including organic disease, may follow some months later or on an anniversary of symbolic importance for the lost relationship. (450)

And so, according to Parkes (451), the most characteristic feature of a survivor's grief is not his depression, but his separation anxiety, acute episodic pangs followed by searching. Parkes describes a grief pang as "an episode of severe anxiety and psychological pain." At times when these pangs occur, the close but now dead friend, lover, spouse or other relative is missed terribly and the survivor sobs deeply and cries for that person. The bereaved person will recall, accurately or inaccurately, the many ways in which his life was bound up in that of the dead person, and those activities will seem pointless in the light of recent events (452) or, perhaps, especially charmed. These grief pangs will begin soon after bereavement, and they will be most intense in from 5 to 14 days. Early on, they are frequent and spontaneous, but later they arise only when something happens that brings memories of the loved person to mind (453, 454). Various later events can set off episodes of anxious pining, but the response is to be expected primarily in the first 2 weeks.

Pining is a desire both "persistent and obtrusive" for the person who is no longer here; Parkes says that it is a preoccupation with extremely painful thoughts (455). Pining is "the subjective and emotional component of the urge to search for a lost object." Many social animals search for things they have lost. The human does this in the early stage of bereavement. "The more open the yearning, the healthier it is; the more repressed or otherwise disguised, the more pathological" (456).

With the pining and yearning come sensations of panic, of dry mouth, heavy sighing responses, apparent aimlessness, hyperactivity, difficulties of concentration, recollections of events preliminary to the death, deteriorated interest in persons or activities that typically provide pleasure or attention (457). Unfortunately, there does not seem to be a sharp end-point to the yearning process, and the grief

104

pangs can recur years after a significant death. It also seems to be true that yearning lessens while longing lasts.

According to Bowlby, yearning and reproach which are openly and appropriately expressed will not persist, but when these strong feelings are displaced, they may remain present unconsciously and "rumble on over the years," causing distress to the mourner and to those who are close to him (458).

Searching. Parkes tells us that one of the ways of mitigating the pain of grief is to try to keep from thinking of the dead person and even to stay away from persons and even from environments with a potential for provoking reminiscence (459). Most bereaved people will do this to some extent during the first month of bereavement, Parkes says, but the behavior rarely lasts as long as a year.

A more typical defense is to engage in a search for the "lost" individual. Bowlby (460) held the view that striving to recover the lost object is, in fact, the first stage of the grief syndrome. Parkes explains that for a time the survivor must defend himself against the full reality of what has happened so he denies it and engages in a search for the dead person (461).

Parkes says there are several components of the search. First, there is alarm, tension, and arousal in the grieving person. Second, the grieving person will exhibit restless movement (462). Third, he will be preoccupied with thoughts of the dead person. Fourth, the grieving individual will develop a "perceptual set" for that dead person, a mental image which is necessary to establish recognition when the "lost" individual is eventually seen. Fifth, there will be diminished interest in one's appearance. Sixth, the grieving person will direct attention toward places where the "lost" person might be. Finally, the person in the searching stage of grief will often call out for the "lost" person.

Parkes and others have quoted the psychiatrist, Lindemann, who described grief as follows in his classic 1944 paper:

The activity throughout the day of the severely bereaved person shows remarkable changes. There is no retardation of action and speech; quite to the contrary, there is a rush of speech, especially when talking about the deceased. There is restlessness, inability to sit still, moving about in an aimless fashion, continual searching for something to do. There is, however, at the same time, a painful lack of capacity to initiate and maintain normal patterns of activity. (463)

But Parkes denies that the "aimless" moving about is aimless at all—it is for the purpose of finding the "lost" person—but the grieving person probably does not recognize or admit that is what he is doing and to explain the restless activity he will call it "aimless."

The search is buying time for the bereaved person and thus it is facilitative. It helps keep him from having to work right away with a terrible reality; it gives him time to get things together (464) and lets him enact the most common behavior exhibited by social animals when something is lost: searching (465). The behavior has been observed among greylag geese (466) and has been reported as common among other birds and mammals, especially dogs (467). Bowlby has held that weeping and "aggressive thought and action" (such as searching) are appropriate and functional responses when a thing is temporarily lost, and thus are to be expected as initial reactions at a time of bereavement loss (468).

Parkes says it is probable that any bereaved human knows it is pointless to search for someone who is known to be dead, but this does not deter the apparently inevitable compulsion to search (469). However, because he understands on a cognitive level that searching is a senseless exercise, he will resist when told what he is doing. Bereaved people usually do not know on a *thinking* level that they have a need to search (470). The impulse comes from the *feeling* level, but it is evidently very real. Furthermore, the searching impulse seems to be strongest among parents who have lost their children; thus, the common visits by parents to the graves of their sons killed in wartime, the characteristic feature of young mothers going time and again to the room which belonged to a dead infant. We also find the widower wandering to the kitchen, the widow's frequent visiting of her dead husband's study, adoptive children going to great lengths as adults to find their "real" parents (471).

But searching has broader implications, because that which is sought is often found (472). So there will be illusions of "seeing" the dead person when actually it is someone else, of "hearing" the dead person when the sound is really something else. These are not signs of psychopathology; they are normal; they are perceptual near-misses which happen when people are "searching." These kinds of experiences are common, but people often do not know this, and they need to be reassured that the illusions are normal and to be expected (473).

This illusion of seeing or hearing the dead person, the sense that he somehow remains very close, is the most common means of mitigating the pain of grief (474). The sensation is not at all a spooky one but one which provides comfort. Other commonly reported hallucinations include both the visual and auditory. They encompass conversations with the dead person and sensations of being touched by that person (475). Apparently the phenomenon is a particularly strong one among Hopi Indians, especially among their older women (476). The pining individual may experience a strong and warming feeling of the "lost" person's presence, but then recognize it is only an illusion and return once more to the pining (477).

> *Grief fills the room up of my absent child,*
> *Lies in his bed, walks up and down with me,*
> *Puts on his pretty looks, repeats his words,*
> *Remembers me of all his gracious parts,*

Stuffs out his vacant garments with his form:
Then have I reason to be fond of grief.

SHAKESPEARE
KING JOHN

Grieving people typically are preoccupied with thoughts of the dead person and with events leading up to the loss. The memories are remarkable for their clarity and are very intense. One "sees" and is perhaps preoccupied by the dead person as if in life (478, 479). One feels that person, one experiences, as if it were real, that person's vivid presence (480). The reason, again, is that when we search for a thing, we must have a clear mental picture of the thing we are looking for so we will know it when we see it. This is why, during the searching phase, we experience such vital mental pictures of the deceased person. That is the picture of the deceased person. That is the picture of the close person we have "lost," and we want to *find* that person. It is why we so readily misidentify other people as the loved one who has died.

Parkes and others have found that memory of the dead person seems to increase in clarity through the first year postbereavement although occasionally someone will report an inability to recall the face of the dead person during the first month of bereavement (481, 482). It is common for widows to dream of their dead husbands as if they were still living, and in these dreams it is common too for there to be an especially vivid quality of happiness with him, but in these pleasant dreams there may be a lurking suspicion that all is not as it should be (483).

In 1949, Anderson anticipated transactional analysis by giving his impression that when a survivor's remembered relationship with some dead person is "good and adult," the dreams of those interactions will be other than "ferocious," but that nightmares will follow the death of one with whom an "infantile relationship" was shared. In 1962 Krupp reported that the dreams of widows who had had happy marriages were happy dreams, whereas nightmares of anger, fright, and attack greeted widows whose marriages were characterized by hostility or ambivalence. And it is interesting to note Parkes' report that widows with strong illusional experiences concerning their dead husbands have fewer sleep disturbances than those widows who have no such illusions (484).

Parkes (485) says it is common during the searching phase to go through the dead person's clothing, perhaps to wear his clothes, to display his personal possessions such as pipes, wallets, pictures, or to give special household status to items such as "his chair." Some families sanctify the missing member and make their home a lasting memorial to the person (486). The bereaved person may feel "an uncanny force" drawing him to the graveyard, and it is not unusual for the survivor to be concerned for the deceased person's comfort at the cemetery if the weather gets bad (487).

> *Warm summer sun, shine kindly here;*
> *Warm southern wind, blow softly here;*
> *Green sod above, lie light, lie light—*
> *Good night, dear heart,*
>
> > *good night, good night.*
>
> > MARK TWAIN
> > (ON THE TOMBSTONE OF SUZY,
> > HIS DAUGHTER)

During the searching phase, too, some people will go to spiritualists, and occasionally they report having had some kind of "contact" with the dead—but there is no evidence that such contacts are helpful in any way. Often, according to Parkes, people who "make contact" with the dead by way of spiritualists are more frightened by the experience than helped by it (488).

Persons who are engaged in the searching process are usually so preoccupied with it that they have few other interests, and there may be few expressed requirements for basic needs such as food, sleep, appearance, work, or family (489).

Parkes says that active calling for the "lost" person is not an essential part of the search, but that it is often a component, and we can expect to hear such calling from bereaved people (490). However, if things go as usual, the anguished pining becomes less intense as time passes, to be replaced by nostalgic and "bittersweet" feelings (491). It was Angelo Patri who remarked in 1938 that: "In one sense there is no death. The life of a soul on earth lasts beyond his departure. You will always feel that life touching yours, that voice speaking to you, that spirit looking out of other eyes, talking to you in the familiar things he touched, worked with, loved as familiar friends. He lives on in your life and in the lives of all others that knew him."

The searching phase must be resolved, Bowlby believed, if normal grief is not to turn into a pathological response (492). Resolution may come automatically or a "crutch" may be employed. It is not uncommon for people to resolve the search by establishing lasting memorials for the "lost" person: parks, scholarships, buildings, tombstones, special trees, and other lasting things can be part of the process of idealization which, in a sense, keeps the dead person around, encountered from time to time, and remembered. Another kind of memorial is that offered by the person who promises in the future "to be what he would have wanted me to be," or to "carry on for him" (493). Pollock suggests that Lenin pursued through life what he thought were idealistic goals to insure immortality of his older brother, a victim of prerevolutionary execution (494). Of whatever kind they may be, we build monuments to end the search through insuring immortality.

> *Woe's me. Methinks I'm*
> *turning into a god.*
> *EMPEROR VESPASIAN*
> *(ON HIS DEATHBED)*

Anger and Guilt

Kubler-Ross says:

> When we lose someone, especially when we have little if
> any time to prepare ourselves, we are enraged, angry, in
> despair; we should be allowed to express those feelings. The
> family members are often left alone as soon as they have
> given their consent for autopsy. Bitter, angry, or just numb,
> they walk through the corridors of the hospital, unable
> often to face the brutal reality. (495)

She also suggests the obvious for mental health workers
and other helpers: when bereaved people are expressing resentment and anger, we should let them ventilate their feelings without being judgmental (496). According to Falek
and Britton, anger is an understandable and reasonable response when a bereaved person's anxious efforts to do
something suitable meet with failure and, thus, frustration
(497).

Irritability and Bitterness. Parkes tells us that irritability
and anger are most likely to be present during the early,
yearning, pining phase of grief and especially in the first
month (498), and that anger is not always present in either
appropriate or displaced forms among adults, although it
seems always to occur in grieving children (499). When
anger occurs, it can approach or meet levels of furious rage,
and it tends to be most pronounced during the first month
and to occur intermittently thereafter, with episodes of depression and apathetic withdrawal occurring between the
anger episodes. These are characterized by absence of open
aggressiveness (500) with strenuous efforts by some to control their powerful anger (501). Parkes explains that to
argue with the gods or with fate is simply a matter of trying to maintain some control over events which are beyond
control and is to be seen as yet another way of expressing
helplessness (502).

Down, down, down into
the darkness of the grave
Gently they go, the beautiful,
the tender, the kind;
Quietly they go, the intelligent,
the witty, the brave.
I know. But I do not approve.
And I am not resigned.
EDNA ST. VINCENT MILLAY
DIRGE WITHOUT MUSIC

Bereaved people may astonish and even frighten themselves with the strength of their angry feelings (503). "Beating the breast, pounding the head, or thrusting the fist through glass are occasional impulsive, aggressive, and self-destructive acts on the part of the person who is suddenly overwhelmed with grief" (504).

The most common form of anger, probably, is a recurring sort of hypersensitivity and even bitterness, coming up from time to time during the first year. Sometimes a tremor will be present, occasionally the grieving person will stutter. He will complain of being in a turmoil, of little things upsetting him, of his "nerves being on edge," and beyond this, irritable and bitter quarreling seems to be unusually frequent (505). During the terminal illness of a child, marriage stress between his parents is common; the helper who is aware of this fact may be sensitive to developing problems within the relationship with which he may be helpful. It's unfortunate that these expressions have to happen within families, but since everyone is bereaved in these situations, it is little wonder that fights emerge and surprising that they do not come up more often (506).

It seems inevitable that middle class persons will seek to assign blame when something has gone wrong. Thus, in death, the survivors blame God or the physician—perhaps uncertain as to which is Which. They will blame themselves, their "carelessness," their forefathers, their own "sinful past," their lack of "True Faith," evil agents in their food and water, old football injuries, or the funeral director. It seems difficult to accept that, for reasons unknown, a person acquired a particular disease or happened to experience a particular accident which caused death (507–511).

It is "practically inevitable and universal" that the bereaved person will express anger toward the dead partner for deserting him; he may say, directly or in effect, "Why did you do this to me?" (512). But according to Kubler-Ross, since none of us likes to admit anger at a deceased person, these emotions are often disguised or repressed, and they prolong the period of grief or show up in other ways (513). It is not up to us to judge such feelings as bad or shameful, Kubler-Ross suggests, but to understand their true meaning and origins as something very human.

Guilt. Typical of the human feelings mentioned above are those of guilt. Paraphrasing Freud, Bowlby (514) described three kinds of guilt which are common in bereavement: 1) large or small responsibility for the death realistically attributable to the bereaved person, 2) neurotic guilt arising from previous wishing that the person were dead, and 3) irrational guilt stemming from an inward-turning of anger initially felt for the deceased person.

Parkes says that bereaved people tend to go over and over the history of the death, apparently in an effort to reassure themselves (and to be reassured) that they had done everything they could to prevent the ultimate event. This seems to be an effort to put things right, Parkes believes, to find some reason behind apparently irrational events, to bring order out of chaos, to restore "faith in the meaning of life" (515). Yet, as Mendelson observed, there is another side: "Sometimes this anger and these reproaches may be realistic. Other people, by their acts of omission or commission, may have actual feelings or acts to blame themselves for" (516).

Consider, for example, the heart attack victim's widow. From her perspective, she was either incautious in allowing her husband to work too hard and smoke and drink too much, or by nagging about these health considerations she "drove him to his death" (517, 518). Her guilt situation is even more difficult if a precarious heart health circumstance were known to be present, or if at any time she had presented him with any emotional stress, or if at any time she withheld emotional support. Guilt opportunities for the widow, here, are virtually limitless even when (as is usually the case) they are baseless, and several researchers have commented on this problem (519–527).

A variety of observations may occur when a child or adolescent has been directly or indirectly responsible, intentionally or not, for the death of a sibling, or when the surviving youngster has received or perceived receipt of blame. Features include depression, anxiety, guilt, suicidal preoccupation, morbid acting out of the death, and denial of responsibility when in fact the survivor was responsible (528). Mendelson points out that: "Even the lost object may, by acts of commission or omission, have made his own death inevitable. But *the more inappropriate such reproaches are, the more pathologic they are.* If they are unrealistically displaced onto third parties, they may assume a paranoid flavor." [italics added] (529, 530)

Suicide is the obvious example, which results in a peculiar configuration of postbereavement events (531–533). These include severe and enduring emotional distress and unusually high levels of guilt among survivors. Schuyler (534) says flatly that the psychological situation of suicide survivors is distinct from that of survivors of natural deaths. A pronounced factor is relative absence of support and sympathy from one's social group. Self-destructive preoccupations are more common than usual, as is an unusually high level of anger, e.g., "The son of a bitch had the last word!" Scapegoating is common in the family, with attendant disruption of its relationships a possibility, although one researcher has found that families can frequently become closer following the suicide of some family member (535). The frantic search for an explanation may set up indefinite postponement of grief resolution (536).

Yet even when there has been no malpractice, no suicide, no negligence by family members, no incaution by the deceased—when there has simply been a death—it seems that guilt will be a prominent feature of the grieving process (537, 538), related commonly to the slights and discourtesies and oversights and social failures that we all commit with each other when we live closely and which we regret intensely when we look back after a death. And beyond this, we have the fact that grieving persons may experience sensations of total exhaustion and inability to perform routine and necessary household tasks, which contributes to the acquisition of yet additional guilt.

Guilt has still another dimension, in which it takes on somewhat different properties in bereavement, and that is when the relationship has been an ambivalent one. An ambivalent relationship—one in which feelings toward some person are opposite and contradictory, e.g., love–hate, respect–jealousy—complicates the guilt reaction. In these cases, guilt will be more pronounced, and guilt in combination with anger can be destructive. So, unusual intensity of anger and guilt, when the relationship was ambivalent, can be seen as a predictor of pathological grief (539, 540). The traditional psychoanalytic view has been that post-bereavement guilt is inward-directed hostility which the grieving person formerly had at an unconscious level for the dead person. Today, Parkes tells us that in ambivalent human relationships, one person wishes (perhaps at a pre-conscious level but certainly at some level which he is unlikely to admit) to hurt the other person or to have him hurt (541), and he may even want (perhaps consciously) the other person to be dead. But when the death wish is gratified, even when no reasonable blame lies with the surviving person, the survivor is left with a terrible load of guilt. He may try to work out his guilt by loud and long mourning, but we should remember too that many people with strong ambivalent feelings may exhibit a delayed grief reaction which has its own complications. Engel (542) believed that ancient superstitions involving ghosts returning to haunt the living and retaliate against them arose out of unresolved guilt from ambivalent relationships. Parkes has found that bereaved psychiatric patients, again and again, return to their guilt over the ambivalent relationship and the death wish, and they see this as their major problem in maintaining satisfactory adjustment. It seems reasonable to suggest that strong feelings of guilt are more likely to emerge following the death of an ambivalently regarded partner than they are from the death of a loved partner. But again, all love includes dimensions of stress, of displeasure, sometimes of anger, certainly of episodes of thoughtlessness, and when the time comes that it is no longer possible to stroke someone's back or say something kind that will be heard, the guilt comes on: "Why didn't I do it *then?*"

Clayton et al. (543) found that the quality of guilt in bereaved persons is different than that characteristic of clinical depressives and tends to focus on perceived omissions and slight negligences. Bereaved persons seem to worry that they did not get the spouse to the hospital sooner, or see the deceased partner before death, or try hard enough to make the marriage satisfying. Kubler-Ross has pointed out that "feelings of love and hate are human and understandable and do not require a gruesome price," yet that is what we seem to demand of ourselves (544).

> A husband and wife may have been fighting for years, but when the partner dies, the survivor will pull his hair, whine and cry louder and beat his chest in regret, fear and anguish, and will hence fear his own death more often than before, still believing in the law of talion—an eye for an eye, a tooth for a tooth—"I am responsible for her death, I will have to die a pitiful death in retribution." If someone grieves, beats his chest, refuses food, tears his hair, it's an attempt at self-punishment to avoid or reduce the anticipated punishment for the blame that he takes on the death of a loved one (545).

Parkes suggests that it is easier to take on oneself the guilt of self-blame than it is to accept the uncertainty of life (546). Consistent with this view is the observation that it is not uncommon for grieving parents to imagine that their own "sins" in younger life were somehow responsible for the present tragedy, their reasoning apparently being that God punishes sinners by murdering their children.

Parkes suggests too that the bereaved person who is expressing lots of guilt and self-reproach should be given special help, since his research shows that these attitudes are common among bereaved persons who go on to develop serious emotional distress (547). If the anger is freely expressed toward its appropriate object, it is likely to fade away (548); if guilt occurs in combination with despair, attitudes of unworthiness, persecution, and ambivalence (549), referral to a psychologist or psychiatrist should be considered.

A special kind of guilt involves persons who have survived a disaster in which multiple lives are lost. Called the "Buffalo Creek Syndrome" (550), after a broken dam episode, the clinical picture involves unresolved grief, psychic numbing, impotent rage, hopelessness, somatic complaints, and *survivor guilt* or *survivor shame* which seems to persist longer than usual bereavement responses (550, 551). The special problems of therapeutic assistance following a disaster have been addressed also by Raphael (552).

Projection of Anger. So, guilt is part of the angry phase— but so is flat-out anger—anger which can be terribly frustrating unless it can be directed against someone. We should remember that *projecting* our distress (psychologically, getting it away from ourselves and onto someone else) is a common form of defense which persons use in various stressful situations. In grief, anger directed toward the physician is common. According to Clayton and his colleagues (553) some 13% of bereaved persons blame either themselves or the attending physician when death happens, again a reason why physicians commonly absent themselves from the family during the moribund period. Reality is that medical negligence contributory to a hospital death is unusual (554). It is true that anger can be taken out against anyone who happens to be handy. The most typical target, particularly of mothers, is likely to be the physician, especially in cases of a child's terminal illness in which the mothers are having unusual difficulty in accepting the impending death (555).

Mendelson says:

> Certainly there is no doubt that loss in childhood produces anger and reproaches in the bereaved child, and that in the adult anger may be directed at the physicians and others responsible for the loss. Self-reproaches may be experienced or expressed for real or imaginary measures that might have been but were not taken to avert the loss or for real or exaggerated mistreatment of the lost love object while he was alive. (556)

Some cultures provide for ritualistic contention with anger in bereavement (557), but these customs are not prevalent in the Western World. Indeed, there is little place for such relief.

Parkes cautions that those who express the most anger seem to wind up being the most lonely and insecure (558); they either drive their friends away or hide from them, and thus it may be the ones who are most angry who need the most objective outside help. Kubler-Ross adds that "The most meaningful help we can give any relative, child or adult, is to share his feelings before the event of death and to allow him to work through his feelings, whether they are rational or irrational" (559).

And we have been reminded by Bowlby that those who attempt, often angrily, to recover the dead person are behaving healthily and in a way which permits eventual emotional disengagement (560). An inability to be freely expressive of such feelings tends to enhance their persistence at some unconscious level so that they are characteristic features of chronic mourning and pathological grief.

Depression and Despair

The grief pang period, the time of separation anxiety with pining, yearning, and searching, is followed in the grief syndrome by a period of apathy, with depressive withdrawal becoming more prominent (561), perhaps, as Falek and Britton (562) believe, as a direct outgrowth of earlier anger and frustration. This is a time when the prevailing affective tone is one of depression and defeat (563), or inertia, purposelessness, and helplessness (564), or apathy (565). It is the "phase of disorganization and despair" (566) although active yearning may still be present and is not unusual (567). The characteristic mood is depression, which is typified by pessimism, withdrawal, sadness, flat affect, loss of aggressiveness, gloom, weeping, reliance on relatives and close friends, loss of interest, and lots of guilt.

One investigation revealed that the affective symptoms of normal, grieving persons one month postbereavement presented so much overlap with the corresponding symptoms of depressed psychiatric patients that the two populations could not be distinguished from each other by their symptoms (568). However, such symptoms seem not to be consistent with the usual neurotic syndromes (569).

> *I'm Smith of Stoke, aged sixty-odd,*
> *I've lived without a dame*
> *From youth-time on; and would to God*
> *My Dad had done the same.*
>
> THOMAS HARDY
> EPITAPH TO A PESSIMIST

Clayton and his colleagues found in 1968 that depressed mood, sleep disturbances, and crying were typical responses to bereavement, with difficulty in concentrating, loss of interest in the environment, and loss of appetite being observed frequently among grieving persons. This period is not a clear-cut phase of grief, according to Parkes, but it seems to occur again and again across the entire grieving period (570) with episodes of what Engel called alternating "flashes of despair and anguish as the reality of the loss briefly penetrates into consciousness." We should remember that one expects to observe depressed mood in bereaved people, and its presence, in and of itself, is not a sign of psychopathology. On the contrary, the absence of depression is more an abnormal sign than its presence (571). It should be borne in mind that the depression of grieving is not normally a full-blown clinical reactive depression. Psychopathology materializes when one extends the sadness of grief to a variety of circumstances extraneous to the grief situation itself and reacts in a grieving-like way to much of his life situation (572, 573).

But we should be familiar with the typical clinical picture of the depressed individual, which will be much the same whether the depression is exogenous or endogenous, physical or psychogenic, normal or psychopathological. Of course, in the case of a grieving depression it is an exogenous event, caused by something outside of the individual's physical system. Again, depression following bereavement is not psychopathological, but the signs of depression are much the same for our purposes. The depressed individual looks unhappy: his expression is melancholic, and in a grief situation the melancholic appearance will probably coincide with retarded activity (as opposed to the agitated behaviors of some depressives). The general appearance is a glum, forlorn, gloomy, dejected one of sadness: corners of the mouth are turned down; there is a furrowed brow, deep lines and facial wrinkles; the eyes are often red from crying, especially among women; and in either sex there will be a hurt look. The person will seem solemn and wearily resigned, and the appearance may even seem frozen in a gloomy expression although there will probably be some lability and even transient genuine smiling or forced social smiling—or mirthless smiling if someone tries to be funny. The depressed person's posture is likely to be stooped and his speech will probably be slow. His attitude will be one of low mood, indecisiveness, hopelessness, and inadequacy (574). The facial, behavioral, and attitudinal signs of depression are so typical that there is no mistaking them, and the face of grief is known the world over.

Still, the best predictor of nonpsychotic depression at 13 months postbereavement is the presence of depression at 1 month postbereavement (575), a presence which Clayton and his associates observed in over a third of widows and widowers whom they studied (576). Arguments have been advanced that there may be a direct causal link, in women, between the loss of a mother before their 11th year and development of difficult depressions in adult life (577, 578). Early parent death does not, however, appear to prognosticate suicide in later life although one small English study revealed significantly higher incidence of suicide among unmarried males within 5 years of parent deaths, particularly in the cases of maternal deaths when emotional distress had been observed in the eventual suicides before their bereavements (579).

Acceptance

The final stage of the grief syndrome is acceptance. This does not mean that the grieving person has accepted the rightness or appropriateness of what has happened but, rather, he has accepted that it happened and it is time to get on with other things. Lopata (580) believes that for widows, grieving is over only when the woman is successful in modifying her identity in social roles and relations. Yet, "getting on with other things" may begin too soon. There are bereaved spouses who rush into crowded social lives, sell their possessions, move precipitously, and perhaps shun old friends (581). It seems likely that these types of behaviors are less indicative of acceptance than of persistent denial and failure to cope with the imperative of grief resolution.

But doing it right is what Freudians call "decathexis": finding other objects to invest with libidinal energies; others have referred to what Engel (582), as an example, described as the bitter and the sweet becoming separated and the grieving person ultimately coming to peace with himself and his new state.

> *Grief melts away*
> *Like snow in May*
> *As if there were no such cold thing.*
> > *GEORGE HERBERT*
> > *THE TEMPLE*

Many months are required for this process and as it is accomplished, the survivor's preoccupation with the dead person progressively lessens. Now, reminders of the dead person less often and more intensely evoke feelings of sadness and more ambivalent memories can be tolerated with less guilt. As the ties are progressively loosened, the earlier yearnings to be with the dead person, even in death, begin more and more to be replaced by a turning to life and a wish to live. Now, the identification with the ideals, wishes and aspirations of the lost object provide an impetus to continue in life, often expressed as a wish "to be what he would have wanted me to be" or "to carry on for him." When successful, this represents a developmental process, an actual growth experience, which may sometimes even contribute significantly to a characterological change in the mourner, as when a son settles down and assumes responsibilities which he had evaded prior to his father's death. (583)

Mendelbaum referred to this as a time when the survivor becomes operational again and is active and responsive to work and recreation, and to his emotional life (584). Freud believed that persons who are unsuccessful in transferring affection felt for the dead person to some other individual will, instead, invest that affection in themselves, with melancholic narcissism resulting. Bowlby, for one, has taken issue with this theory, arguing that it does not account for the persistent striving to recover some "lost" person, which is so commonly observed as to be regarded as a universal behavior in grieving (585).

Parkes points out that the bereaved person's friends normally begin with sympathy, but this sympathy seems to diminish and disappear if the grief is not brought under control, leaving the chronic mourner in isolation (586). So while it is desirable for a bereaved person to mourn his loss, it is also important for the grieving person to come to terms with events as a reasonable amount of time passes. Sometime, the person has to stop the grieving process and begin a rebuilding process. There may very likely come a time, Parkes advises, when a relative, close friend, or helping professional may have to suggest gently that the grieving has gone on long enough, and that it is time to begin attending to other things (587). It may be particularly important that an outsider make this suggestion, since bereaved persons may see prolonged mourning as being some kind of duty; they may believe the rest of the family expects them to continue in mourning forever and ever. It sometimes takes a sensitive outsider to indicate, after a time, that one's appropriate duty has been done and the real world is waiting. Or on occasion a halt must be called for the enactor of "the grieving game" played by the bereaved person who spends inordinate time refusing to cope and instead runs from friend to friend and therapist to therapist with seemingly and apparently very real endless pain and sorrow. This kind of griever is expressing avoidance, to be sure, but he is also receiving lots of what psychologists call "secondary gain," or positive and intensely gratifying personal attention which he believes he would miss were it not for his bereavement.

Typically, interest in food is one of the first postbereavement needs to reemerge (588). When the grieving individual begins to exhibit interest in his future and to plan appropriately for it, one knows that recovery from the grieving is taking place—but this usually happens some time after bereavement.

Pollock (589) believed that as the dead person's belongings are abandoned and one's own residential and life style arrangements are altered, there occurs a realization, perhaps at an unconscious level, that sources of pleasure exist and are available elsewhere. Such sources then come into focus for the survivor and, while they are not precise substitutes, they permit acceptance of the reality of loss and allow the end of mourning.

Some people in grief will fill their lives with activities so that they are continually busy and preoccupied; Parkes (591) says that people who escape in this way usually find themselves working until late at night, on weekends and holidays, and so on—but this is not a true form of acceptance or of getting on with things—it is avoidance. These people who defend themselves by taking up lots of busy activities tend to drop these activities fairly soon because they have trouble concentrating on them.

But turning points arrive. Some widows, Parkes says, report that they reached a turning point when they got around to sorting out their dead husband's clothes (591). Others say a turning point was reached when they repainted the house or rearranged furniture. Turning points can also include the times when a widow takes a vacation, accepts a job, has a date for the first time since bereavement, or re-decorates (592). This is evidence that the widow does not have to continue focusing her life on a search for the dead person, and this is when positive changes come in the direction of restructuring. These turning points have a way of showing up at predictable times such as the date of the wedding anniversary, a birthday, or the death anniversary. The person is likely to sense the turning point at such a time, and that first death anniversary is a particularly good time for the bereaved individual to stop by the cemetery, or for friends to get together for an informal memorial service— either, Parkes says, can be an effective rite of passage. The helper should remember that the first death anniversary and

the first wedding anniversary that one spends alone are full
of meaning and, beyond that, they are the first major events
in a married couple's relationship which have significance
for both but which are not shared by both—and it is a time
when the immediate family may be reliving events of the
death in vivid detail (593, 594). Other important dates may
include birthdays of various family members, and holidays
such as Christmas, Thanksgiving, Mother's Day, and Father's
Day. These can be times when there will be a lot of hurt.
Helpers should be aware that there can be anticipatory grief
in the days leading up to such significant anniversaries and
celebrations, and these can be more troublesome emotionally than the special days themselves.

> *Ah woe is me! Winter is come and gone*
> *But grief returns with the revolving year.*
> *SHELLEY*
> *ADONAIS*

> Complete resolution of the grief is indicated by the ability
> to remember comfortably and realistically both the pleas-
> ures and disappointments of the lost relationship. When
> successful, the survivor becomes capable of carrying on with
> his life and with new relationships, often having profited
> from the positive identification with the lost person. (595)

Scanty available research suggests that when a death situation has produced a mutilated corpse, memories of the
death event are particularly painful, but when the death
has been peaceful and characterized by calm, memories are
likely to be more gentle (596). But even an unpleasant
postmortem memory is probably going to be replaced, over
a period of time, with better memories of the deceased in
happier times (597, 598). This may be part of the reason
we so often observe the survivors idealizing the dead person—
his human but negative characteristics are forgotten, his
"better side" is treasured (599). Survivors may incorporate

into their own behavioral repertoires "certain admired qualities and attributes of the dead person through the mechanism of identification" or endeavor to carry out the lost person's life goals (600). Even a drunken, brutal, irresponsible and shiftless ape of a man is likely to be remembered by his beaten, defeated, and destitute widow as a kindly prince of a giving fellow.

> *By and by*
> *God caught his eye.*
> *DAVID McCORD*
> *EPITAPHS*
> *"THE WAITER"*

III

ᗡ·ᗡ·ᗡ·ᗡ·ᗡ

SURVIVING

ᗡ·ᗡ·ᗡ·ᗡ·ᗡ

T hose who help the bereaved must expect to find that persons who are in grief and who may need their help can be "defensive, sensitive, vulnerable, and unreasonable." At the same time they "need protection, reassurance, time to recoup, and help in developing their blueprints for the future" (601). While various observers have noted that folkway which seems common in the Western world of the widow choosing as her male adviser her dead husband's brother or as a second choice her own brother, Parkes says that someone apart from the immediate family can occupy a unique role which simply is not available to those who are close, "too involved," and too susceptible to the hurt that others, quite unintentionally, may give (602). Parkes notes the existence of family hierarchies which may actually interfere with the open expression of grief by various members as individuals struggle to maintain their status, power, or leadership positions, or actually become competitive with one another as to the magnitude of grief expressed.

Parkes adds that some widows will observe insincere expressions of grief in other family members and will be so turned off by it that they inhibit their own grieving processes simply not to be thought insincere, too (603). Families with these built-in inhibitors may, then, be particularly welcoming to helpful outsiders.

FUNERAL AND RITUAL

We know that grief pangs tend to reach a peak in most people during the second week postbereavement, but the funeral usually takes place within a week—much too soon for the funeral to have maximum psychological benefit (604), too soon for it to constitute something more than a disposal service, to constitute instead a successful rite of passage, to allow for what Nichols and Nichols (605) have called the intellectual and emotional acceptance of death (606–609), a combination of what Prado de Molina (610) has characterized as acceptance of external and internal realities. Often, the value of the funeral is lost on those immediately bereaved, although it does have the effect of bringing the family together at a time when family strength can be helpful (611), and the funeral attracts supporting friends who can share the loss and accept the regressive behaviors of the immediate family (612).

While the funeral symbolizes letting go and saying good-bye, it frequently does not work that way and is really only a beginning. Parkes (613) and others have stated that a major cause of maladaptive behaviors following bereavement—and under influence of personality characteristics and relationship variables—is the absence in today's society of social expectations and rituals which facilitate mourning—which, among other things, pronounce the reality of death and serve to make that fact clear—an understanding which is psychologically necessary in the successful grieving process (614). As Engel put it: "The viewing of the body, the lowering of the casket, and the various rituals of different religious beliefs allow for no ambiguity. Furthermore, this experience takes place in a group, permitting ordinarily guarded feelings to be shared and expressed more readily" (615).

There seems to be consensus that the absence of such traditional rituals and rites is, at least, a contributor to profound emotional distress. Various social conventions connected with mourning may objectively and dispassionately be considered absurd—but, despite their foolishness to the rational eye, they have one advantage: they work. They serve "ultimately to detach the grieving person from the dead and to restore him to his place as a member of the social community" (616). Nichols and Nichols say:

It has been our experience (as funeral directors) in situations of sudden and unexpected death, childhood deaths, or expected deaths where the preparatory grief work is unfinished, that the grief needs of the survivors are frequently acute and a death observance that will promote opportunity to actualize the loss, to express real feelings, and to feel community support will address itself more specifically to the grief work (than will a dispassionate memorial service). If the observance includes some level of involvement and participation among survivors, then it will facilitate and focus on the grief work. (617)

However, it should be added that if we are going to have funerals, we ought to apply what we know of psychological healing and make the funeral ritual more meaningful than it is at present. It could be psychologically helpful rather than being a mere theological ritual with certain side benefits; it could be what Nichols and Nichols have idealized as a time of participation rather than a mere spectator observation (618). (For a remarkable story of parent involvement and participation in the funeral of a child, see Nichols and Nichols, 1975, pp 94–95, in re Keith.) We could do this by, first, setting the funeral at a later time than it is normally scheduled, when that is culturally and religiously possible, perhaps during the second week after the death has occurred—and by scheduling a memorial service one year after the death.

Should children attend funerals of close persons, relatives, parents? The answer depends largely on the child's needs and on what he himself wishes to do. As Gyulay (619) has pointed out, the funeral can never be more scary than the child's own fantasies of it. If a decision is made for the child to attend, he should stay in the company of some known and trusted adult who can explain before the service what is going to happen and describe during it what is going on. Some adults, given charge of children in funerals, have forced the children to kiss or touch the dead body. The practice is ghastly if it is compelled by someone in a fit of inappropriate endearment; if the gesture is spontaneous and from the child, the macabre element is missing and presumably little harm will result. Some judgment and knowledge of the particular child are called for in making this decision, and much of the answer depends on assessing the needs of the particular individual.

It does seem that a word is in order, here—if you will, a lengthy parenthetical observation—about the funeral director. The courtesy is deserved.

North American funeral directors have managed to get a "bad press" for themselves, thanks in large measure to the frightful and grossly inappropriate conduct of a small percentage of their number, and advertising in certain of the industry's trade journals which has been remarkably crass, insensitive, and tasteless when read by persons outside the industry for whom such sales messages have not been intended. While it is true that the funeral is, after one's home and car, the most expensive endeavor in which he is likely to be involved, it is also true that traditional funerals require lots of people (who are on salary), lots of space (which must be paid for), lots of equipment (on which there is probably a bank debt), lots of activity which people want. And it is also true that funeral directors, as a group, are not all that bad.

As a matter of fact, most may even be dedicated persons with a strong sense of professional commitment and commendable ethical values. The profit margins of American funeral homes are lower than those of most successful businesses, and the small advantages of overselling caskets (as one example) would not make sense, immediately or in the long run. It is important to remember too that a large percentage of North American funeral homes are family enterprises which, in many cases, have survived for generations—a history which would be uncharacteristic of any community business with an earned reputation for cheating, trampling grieving widows, stealing insurance, or losing track of bodies. The grey and ghoulish spectre seen shambling down a dark back street in a frayed black suit is more likely to be a contemporary university professor than a mortician.

A number of funeral directors are reputed to be loved by their dogs, if not by their children. Their own emotionality at times of personal grief is likely to be more profound than that which they routinely observe. Few emulate Digby O'Dell in promising Rotary brethren to be "the last friend to let you down."

The funeral director is a person who is in business, to be sure, and who performs a carefully described social function which his community requires, and nearly always, that function is performed honorably and well. The funeral director is the person who is present when there is need, who knows what to do, and who does it with tack and concern. He (or she!) recognizes that the calling does not generate the warmest regard in a society which condemns death, and in a quiet moment between engagements may ask only that his lapses and those of his colleagues be taken in context, and that not all be condemned for the grotesqueries of a few.

Parkes says that a traditional mourning period is helpful to the bereaved and also gives important social cues to others who interact with them, as exemplified by the "signals" transmitted by black armbands and dark dresses (620). These tokens provide indication of how the bereaved person may behave, what may be expected of him, and how he should be treated during his trouble. The mourning period has a further advantage of helping the mourner to accept rather than to avoid his depression.

But one does not see mourning dress and black armbands any more except perhaps in observances which are symbolic at a level once removed from the original symbolism intended by, as one example, armbands.

Along with the absence of symbols of mourning, it is also rare that a family dresses its own dead members for the funeral. One sees bright colors; one hears brittle chatter. One leaves details to the funeral director. One observes and practices avoidance.

The relative absence of supporting social rituals contributes to the loneliness and isolation spouses experience in the months following bereavement and may stimulate a resurgence of anxiety, dejection, and despair 4 to 6 months after the death (621).

Grief passes, but the facilitative helper should not tell a bereaved person that his grief will pass; he will only annoy that person and get the indignant response he deserves. Nor should the helper tell a grieving person to stop grieving before he is ready to do so; that time will come, in most cases, but it shouldn't be pushed. One shouldn't move in before the grieving person is ready.

Our tasks with the ending of grief are more complex than they have been at other times and in other societies, because here the behaviors are very much up to the individual, within a framework which has been established by research and clinical observation but which he probably does not know about. The helper can use his knowledge to *help*. One who knows what the stages are can provide that help.

And while we are on the subject, let's notice too that, if a person knows what the grief stages are, when his own time for grieving comes he will know what to expect. However, once the stages of grief are learned, there is the danger that he will consider himself too learned to go through them. That would be a mistake; any person, no matter how learned, should go through the stages. The person who is informed as to what they are and what they are not may find the trip more interesting, but he should not try to avoid the adventure. The helper too, be he a friend, a professional, or both, should allow himself to be human—the helper is not immune from the harm that can come from avoidance of strong affect.

A TIME TO RECOUP

The bereaved person, at least during the early days, is likely to need assistance from others with even the most simple decisions (622). The person also needs time for himself, he has to begin to organize his ideas and understand truly what has happened. So an immediate task of close persons is to help the bereaved person take care of those tasks that must be done, then look after him. It may be necessary to protect the bereaved person for a time from neighbors and friends, but caution has to be exercised here since the bereaved person needs to know he has friends and they should not be driven away or antagonized. During the first few hours, anyway, a tactic can be one of getting the "helpful others" busy doing some of the necessary practical things. When the bereaved person's initial numbness wears off, that person will be better equipped to contend with condolences and other matters (622).

Parkes reminds us that a grieving widow with children to care for is under considerable stress and is in particular need of helpful outsiders to help with the children—who also have grieving to do (623). Adult children and near-adult children can help the grieving widow or widower, too. Their support seems to be particularly helpful. It is not altogether clear which is the caregiver and which the cared-for in these circumstances, but the shared grief is the important thing psychologically (624). Parkes adds that the most help to a grieving person seems to derive from "quiet communication of affectionate understanding" (625). A squeeze of the hand, Parkes suggests, may be lots better than the mum-

bling of pious conventionalities, and someone who can provide a warm and understanding presence may set up the
desirable vacuum from frenzied activity into which the
grieving person may be expressive of his strong feelings.

VISITORS

From a psychological point of view, persons who are not
immediately close should not be calling at the home during
the first 24 hours after bereavement (626) since survivors
are still in a state of shock and they are not ready yet to
contend with anything, let alone a houseful of people want-
ing and trying to be helpful. But here we have to keep in
mind the Jewish exception. Orthodox members of that
faith will be interested in a burial which is substantially
more rapid than is common among Christians. The cultural
rituals are established and include early visits, assumption
of various set duties by family members, and the like.

Parkes suggests in his *Studies of Bereavement* that house
visits following bereavement tend to be frustrating for everyone because the visitor cannot bring back the person who
has died and the bereaved person cannot help the visitor by
seeming to have been helped (625). It is a no-win situation
for both and it is painful for both, and more than one person has noticed that in such situations it often turns out to
be the bereaved widow or widower who ends up trying to
comfort those who have come to call.

People coming into a house of bereavement typically do
not know what to say. They are often told not to upset
the widow, and even without these instructions they may
find conversation difficult—conventional babble is clearly
inappropriate, and they probably think that by avoiding
mention of what has happened they can avoid grief entirely.

But still, what does one say? Rabbi Stuart Davis suggests
that the reason we avoid talking in *significant* ways with
mourners is so that we will not have to confront our own
feelings, so that we will not have to confront "our own

finitude." The best course, apparently, is to convey some conventional expression of sympathy but to avoid the sepulchral tone and to avoid pity, which is the last thing the bereaved person wants—he does not want to be a pitied object. (There may be exceptions.) The visitor should usually feel free to say what he has on his mind, or say nothing at all. But he may as well forget the trite formulas; they do not help particularly and serve only to observe social ritual and fill the air with noise.

> *Great grief will not be tould,*
> *And can more easily be thought than said.*
> > *EDMUND SPENSER*
> > *THE FAERIE QUEENE*

It is probably more appropriate to be less concerned with what one says than to attend carefully to what *the bereaved person is trying to say.* "People need to be encouraged to talk about the person who died," according to Nichols and Nichols (627), to remember him, to share about him. Psychotherapy (the helper in bereavement is providing a psychotherapeutic relationship) is based on the idea that the helper's attentive and accurate listening is vastly more significant in the outcome than is his knowledgeable talking. So, the question "What does one say?" is probably better stated as *"How can one best hear?"*

And the helper should not say, "Call me when you feel up to it." The helper means it, but the bereaved person will have heard this a hundred times and probably does not want even the gentlest of obligations. The *helper* should call, or better, should get busy in a nonobtrusive way in working with some of the many details which will be actively of assistance to the grieving person.

It has been traditional for clergymen to visit parishioners during terminal illness and to try comforting the bereaved thereafter, but many clergymen are just as uncomfortable in the grief situation as is anyone else (628–630). They find little magic in words that do not add much. Many simply do not make the gesture of calling any more unless they are personally acquainted with persons in the situation. One study found that widows experienced little postbereavement help from religion (631). There is other evidence, however, that grieving persons have appreciated a clergyman's call, particularly if he has evidenced genuine concern and has not just been taking advantage of the bereaved person's grief to proselytize (632, 633). Parkes believes that a visit by the right clergyman in the right frame of mind is appreciated.

The week after the funeral is perhaps the best time for the clergyman (and other postbereavement helpers) to call. Visits should be planned to occur at a variety of times across the first year. It ought to be added that if the clergyman is a close friend or an intimate of the family it can well be appropriate—even an imperative—for him to come much sooner and to behave as any other close and bereaved person. No one should expect him to behave in those circumstances as an objective and clinically detached professional, and he should not expect that kind of behavior of himself.

Parkes (634) suggests that a particularly helpful time for people to assist is during the few days after the funeral, when social conventions have been exhausted and survivors are in an even more difficult stage of bereavement than they were at the time of death (635). That is the time when the family has dispersed and bereaved survivors are apt to be left alone. They are likely to be experiencing the height of their grief at this time and having lots of things to contend with. Kubler-Ross agrees: "The void and emptiness is felt after the funeral, after the departure of the relatives. It is at this time that family members feel most grateful to have someone to talk to... This helps the relative over the shock and the initial grief and prepares him for a gradual acceptance" (636).

Parkes believes that grieving persons appreciate it when others stop by to offer condolences, because these visits are seen as tributes to the dead and they confirm the mourner's belief that the pain is worthy and valid. Also, and maybe more importantly, according to Parkes, house visits reassure the bereaved that they are not alone and reduce anxiety and insecurity (637). The first month seems to be a particularly difficult time, characterized by crying, depressed mood, and sleep disturbances (638). The visits may help make the world seem less "dangerous and alien," (639) because allies are present and it is with them that the photo album is bound to be shared.

BOLD FACES

Parkes points out that there are strong social pressures for bereaved persons to wear "bold faces" during the funeral proceedings (640). Once these proceedings are out of the way, however, he believes persons should be left pretty much to follow their own needs. Significant others can be invaluable by being around the home to keep the household functioning and looking after the bereaved persons' needs. Such persons may catch a lot of flak from the bereaved, who will be taking out their anger and frustration on everyone in sight—and perhaps particularly the outsider—but that is part of being the helper in a grief situation. In fact, a helper can be particularly useful at this time by encouraging the ventilation of grieving persons' feelings; he may prevent profound or at least long-lasting complications which can arise from unresolved grief.

Most people are psychologically naive, and may believe that to "break down" in times of adversity such as bereavement has something to do with what laymen call "nervous breakdown." There is, of course, no connection, any more than there is such a thing as nervous breakdown—people's nerves do not break down although sometimes the capacity for normal functioning does. *People who can express strong emotion are less likely to go into psychological collapse during bereavement or later than are persons who feel compelled*

to bottle up their feelings. We have known this for a long
time from psychological research, and Parkes has reported
evidence that bereaved persons, in particular, who fail to express their distress and emotionality within the first week
or two of bereavement are more likely than others to become emotionally disturbed at a later time (641). The
process is painful, yes—and there is little that even the professional helper can do to eliminate the pain, but in encouraging grief work he can help avoid the possibility of delayed
grief, which is much more painful. What grieving persons
want during mourning may not always be what they need
(642), and what they want may typically be someone's
permission to "break down," a response which many persons may have learned is somehow bad form or, worse, im-
moral. But as Counselor Henry Font has remarked, "Feelings don't know about morality."

At the same time, among those who are willing to express
affect, it is common to hear expressions of fright stimulated
by the intensity of grief feelings and imaginings. Some
grieving persons may believe they are losing their minds, to
believe they are about to have one of those nervous break-
downs. It is appropriate in these circumstances for the
skillful helper to reassure such people—and one can be quite
explicit—and to convey by attitude that the strong feelings
are not distressing, alarming, surprising, or frightening to
the helper (643).

Some of those who think they are "going mad" are those
who are expressing intense anger or bitterness; but also,
people in grief experience hallucinations, and it is commonly thought (most incorrectly) that people who "see
things" are less than emotionally healthy. So, people who
are experiencing this kind of distress should be reassured
that the phenomena are normal. Parkes describes other
typical reactions which are common in grief but perhaps
unexpected by the grieving person: nightmares, nocturnal
orgasms, distractibility, difficulty in remembering routine
matters, a sense of unreality (644). None of these experiences, in and of itself, is a sign that anything psychologically

abnormal is happening—all of these experiences are typical in the grief situation. Above all, according to Kubler-Ross, the helper should "let the relatives talk, cry, or scream if necessary; let them share and ventilate, but be available" (645).

THE HELPER

There is often a sadness about the event of death itself, even when the helper has no personal involvement with the persons associated with that life. There can be a sadness about the circumstances, an empathy for the persons involved, the children, the waste, whatever—that can cause even the objective, well-defended outsider to be genuinely moved by what is happening in the lives of other people. That's okay. According to Parkes (646), bereaved persons take comfort from seeing that those who are near are not afraid to let their own feelings in the situation emerge; it tends to reduce the sense of isolation and let the grieving person know he is not alone. The counselor, though, who is supposed to be a professional—unless he is intimately and personally involved in the grieving situation himself—should not be falling apart and behaving inconsolably. The counselor can be one person in the close situation who has his head on straight, who can maintain an objective view, who can see that things get done without interference from his own emotionality.

> *Everyone can master a grief but he who has it.*
>
> *SHAKESPEARE*
> *MUCH ADO ABOUT NOTHING*

The professional counselor in a grief situation can reassure the persons most directly involved that they are not losing their minds, he can listen and allow ventilation of strong affect, he can perhaps reassure the young woman that she is not a bad mother if she has difficulty coping with her children during the grieving time, he will know what is normal and usual in grief and be able to offer assurance that what is going on is typical (but not in such a way as to seem to minimize the hurt). If abnormalities occur he can make an appropriate referral. But most of all, he can offer a calm presence and availability at a variety of times through the bereavement period and offer a special kind of skilled help for those who need it.

One does not need to be a professional in some mental health area to provide assistance for grieving people. The skilled professional does not need at all times to enact that role. Anyone who cares can be useful. An initimate friend, however that term is appropriately applied, seems to be enormously important in grief (647).

Any surviving spouse needs a helping hand from time to time, but it may be particularly helpful for a surviving husband, whose household skills may be crippled at best through his own socialization, to know that one night a week he can get away from those overwhelming household responsibilities. It may be helpful for some widows to have someone they can call on to repair the plumbing or fix a screen or get the car serviced. The list of ways in which people can be helpful is virtually endless, and the opportunities are available to those who are willing to give it the time.

SPECIAL CONSIDERATIONS

A number of special considerations which do not fit very well elsewhere are important to understanding of bereavement. These will be discussed here. They include physical health, drug usage, psychopathology, suicide, sexual activity, making things easier for survivors, and a note of professional concern for mental health workers.

Physical Health

It seems that physicians, generally, are not seen by bereaved persons as being particularly helpful, except, perhaps, as purveyors of drugs for the symptomatic relief of psychological distress (648). The Parkes studies of widows (649) reveal that widows under age 65 consult their physicians regularly during the first 6 months of bereavement, but widows over 65 do not do so with any greater regularity than they did before bereavement. Young widows between ages 18 and 46, especially those whose husbands died suddenly, are significantly more restless than middle aged and older widows (650). According to Parkes (651), widows under 65 take seven times as many sedatives after as they did before bereavement, but widows over 65 exhibit no increase in the consumption of such drugs. Younger widows think of themselves as being sick; older widows think of themselves as being well. Bereavements in old age can still cause profound grief reactions, but the odds say that death is more acceptable, and bereavements more tolerable, among those who have lived longer. Interestingly, there are research data which indicate that elderly persons whose spouses have died suddenly experience fewer illness symptoms than do those elderly persons whose spouses died after lengthy illnesses (652).

During the first year of bereavement (653), widows exhibit various physical symptoms in excess of the norm: headaches, dizziness, fainting spells, blurred vision, skin rashes, excessive sweating, indigestion, swallowing difficulty, vomiting, heavy menstrual periods, frequent infections, and general aches and pains. Frederick (654) has added that infections and tumors seem to occur with unusual frequency shortly after bereavement. One study of Navajo bereavement revealed that vague aches, pains, and other somatic distress are frequently observed in a culture which prohibits mourning after 4 days and includes sanctions against expressions of anger in circumstances of bereavement (655).

Carey (656) reports that a year after bereavement, widowed men and women are less well adjusted than those who remain married to living spouses. Parkes says that as long as 2 years after their bereavement, widows tend to report poorer health than do married women of the same age (657). The complaints most commonly involve headache, digestive upset, rheumatism, and asthma.

In their study of young American widows and widowers under age 45, Parkes and Brown (658) found that characteristic difficulties included problems of appetite and sleep together with increased use of tobacco, alcohol, and tranquilizers. Bereaved young persons were more frequently hospitalized than were nonbereaved controls, and acute physical symptoms were particularly evident among male survivors. Two to four years postbereavement, few differences in health were observed between bereaved and nonbereaved men and women.

During the first year of bereavement, widows consulted their physicians with vastly increased enthusiasm, complaining particularly of nervousness, depression, fears of "nervous breakdown," feelings of panic, persistent fears, "peculiar thoughts," nightmares, insomnia, trembling, loss of appetite, weight loss, and fatigue. These are all characteristics of normal grief and of anxiety neurosis and anxiety reaction (659); but, beyond that, the information should be considered in a broader context. At least 70% and probably far more, of nonbereaved persons who consult general medical practitioners do so with problems which are *psychological* in character, and with which they are turning to the wrong person for help. True enough, people among this 70% feel ill and believe themselves to be so, but their feelings are symptomatic of underlying emotional distress which creates the discomfort experienced by them as physical. Given this reality among the normal, usual, and nonbereaved general population, the compounding difficulties in a time of grief are obvious. As an example, Smith (660) found that widows with the greatest depression were also those with the largest number of somatic complaints.

During the first year following bereavement, bereaved persons may have a higher mortality rate than do the non-bereaved, but the cause is not known. In the case of sudden and unexpected deaths, the higher mortality rate of survivors during the first year postbereavement is attributed by some to the relatively more severe stress that sudden death imposes (661, 662), or to the sense of worthlessness and of "nothing more to live for" that is commonly experienced by those who care for a person most directly during the final illness (663). Others simply deny that the data justify saying the mortality rate for bereaved persons is higher than for members of nonbereaved groups (664, 665). However, most of the illnesses which precipitate death among mourning persons are attributable to heart disease, especially coronary thrombosis and arteriosclerotic heart disease—this seems to be particularly true during the first 6 months following bereavement. But it is not known if bereavement can cause some illnesses; it may simply aggravate an existing condition—or bereaved people may smoke too much or alter their diets in such a way that disease is brought on. It is all highly speculative (666).

The Parkes studies reveal that the mortality rate among widows and widowers is higher than among married men and women of the same age, but 1) the same is also true of life-long bachelors and spinsters, and 2) the more able-bodied widows and widowers may remarry, which would suggest that those who remain unmarried after the spouse's death may be people with a higher risk of early death. And yet, the death rate among widowers of 54 years and older during the year following bereavement is about 40% higher than would be expected; those who survive the first year seem to experience the same mortality rate as married men of the same age. The death rate among bereaved persons during the first year is on the order of seven times that for nonbereaved persons of the same age (667–672).

Drugs

While there may be merit in going along with the use of some drugs on occasion to provide symptomatic relief for grieving persons (673-675), it is not a good idea to let drugs become a habitual source of comfort. In bereavement they may offer relief, but they do not cure. It is necessary for the person to go through the pain of grief, apparently, if he is going to get his grief work done, and anything that suppresses the natural expression of grief can only be expected to prolong the course of mourning—as best we now understand the process. As a case in point: A young marine's wife was murdered. The marine was put under sedation by physicians and kept drugged for some 50 days. Subsequently, he was discharged as unfit for military service and 5 years later was still trying to handle his grief. It's no wonder.

The message is that drug usage after bereavement should be permitted only with caution although one study revealed that over half of bereaved spouses do use sleep or "nerve medicines" during mourning (676). Another investigator found that widows' greatest help in grief was via symptomatic drugs (677).

The common sorts of drugs taken by bereaved people include sedatives for sleep (and this would include, for this purpose, alcohol), tranquilizers for anxiety, and antidepressive drugs to boost mood. Physicians give these things out because they are quicker than spending the time that is really necessary to be helpful. However, one cannot complain about the judicious use of drugs because no one can say if they are especially harmful or especially good. We do not know if drugs minimize the pain of grief or if they just postpone it. Sometimes the use of drugs for one reason or another is clearly indicated, if just to let a bereaved person get a good night's sleep.

Parkes says that the chance of habituation following drug usage in management of grief is low (678). He cites research evidence showing that in a population of bereaved

widows, of those who were taking drugs during the first
6 months of bereavement, only about 25% were still taking
drugs 1 to 1½ years later, and each of those had been a drug
user prior to bereavement.

Psychopathology

The number of bereaved persons who are admitted to
psychiatric hospitals within 6 months of bereavement is
about six times greater than the number which could be
expected by chance alone, according to the Parkes studies
(679), and in a report by several investigators of emotional
impact on families of childhood death from leukemia. In
over half of families (11 of 20) one or more members required postbereavement assistance for emotional difficulties
from professional mental health workers (680). The most
common diagnosis was reactive depression or neurotic depression, and these diagnoses were twice as common among
recently bereaved patients as among nonbereaved patients.
In many of these cases, the persons were still experiencing
grief as long as a year postbereavement. In their situations,
the emotional disorder seems to represent a pathological
grief expression.

Signs of potential psychopathology among bereaved persons include a) pronounced ideas of guilt or self-reproach,
b) prolonged grief, and c) delayed grief. Delayed grief suggests that a period of 2 or more weeks has elapsed between
the death and the onset of grief pangs, but in some cases
persons do not even acknowledge that there was an initial
period of numbness (681).

The counselor or other helper should watch for characteristics indicating that the grieving process is not going as
it should. Such characteristics, according to the Parkes
studies (682), include the absence of grief when its expression would be appropriate and expected, episodes of panic
or of unusual anger, physical symptoms which persist, inappropriate or excessive guilt, marked self-reproach, or the
presence of strong emotion beyond time limits which are

regarded as normal. Guthiel (683) noted that "old psychiatric experience" regarded as pathologic any grieving which goes on beyond 6 months; despite the viewpoint of old psychiatrists, grieving can go on within "average" boundaries for a year and often more, and psychosis is a very rare result of bereavement. However, special help may be needed for those who handle their grief badly, who persevere in some phase of grieving, or who just do not seem to be coming along as they should (684). The helper should not hesitate to get additional help when he is in doubt.

Atypical grieving includes panic attacks, persisting and intense guilt, or a hypochondriacal or hysterical condition in which the client develops symptoms closely resembling the symptoms suffered by the dead person during his last illness (685). (Engel suggested in 1964 that symptoms of this sort are normal and not uncommon, if their appearances are brief.) Panic attacks include choking sensations, breathless attacks, and somatic expressions of fear. There may be attacks of trembling, with palpitations, sweating, and stomach pains. Depression, tension, and agitation may be reported. The panic attacks are likely to be tied to intense separation anxiety and strong but only partially successful attempts to avoid grieving. In atypical grieving, the underlying separation anxiety seems to be severe. The guilt reaction is intense and can range from feelings of self-reproach related to the widow's idea that she could have done more for her dying husband to conviction that one was directly responsible for the death of a loved person. Many people experiencing guilt also project blame on the physicians, nurses, and others who attended the moribund patient, including members of the family. It is not uncommon for bereaved persons to have guilt for one reason or another concerning lapses in their behaviors toward a dead person during life, but when this guilt and self-reproach are intense, it is a danger signal, warning of possible psychopathology. Hypochondriacal symptoms in grief that suggest psychopathology have to do with aches and pains in the body at the site of pain that had been prominent in the loved person's terminal illness. Pains can simulate coronary thrombosis, lung cancer, injuries related to car accidents, stroke, recurrent vomiting, or paralysis (686).

There are some signs which are typical of endogenous depression for which the helper might look, since their presence would suggest a more profound difficulty than that usually encountered in normal grieving. These signs include noticeable mood fluctuations; a "significant and progressive" loss of weight; precordial anxiety; dry mouth, lack of appetite; constipation; dry skin; and "stubborn and often intractable" insomnia (687). They are rarely observed in psychogenic depression and when observed, require medical or psychiatric referral.

There is some evidence that children who lose a parent early in life, particularly if it is the mother, will be predisposed to clinging behaviors and to excessive grief later in life (688). Other researchers have found that loss of a parent early in life may be a factor in the later development of a severe depression, and still others caution that the failure to work through one's grief adequately can have psychopathological aftereffects (689–692).

The most profoundly distressed widows, including those who require mental hospitalization, are those whose previous life experiences have included losses to which there were excessively severe reactions. Previous excessive grief and depression prognosticate a poor outcome following bereavement (693).

When there have been major stresses during the 2 years before bereavement, there is more likely to be a pathological reaction or poor general adjustment later than if there have been no such stresses (694). The same may be true if there have been episodes of depressive disturbance in the past (695).

Bereaved persons who are most likely to experience profound difficulty are those who, following bereavement, become social isolates: those who are least likely to experience profound difficulty are those who interact actively with family and friends and do the necessary grief work (696).

Suicide

Ideas of suicide are common in bereavement, but they are rarely acted on. The reasons for suicide usually have something to do with ideas of reunion with the dead and for escape from alienation and misery (697).

> *Strew on her roses, roses,*
> *And never a spray of yew.*
> *In quiet she reposes:*
> *Ah! would that I did too!*
> *MATTHEW ARNOLD*

Parkes believes that psychiatric referral is indicated if there is an apparent suicide risk. The helper should not be afraid to ask a direct question about suicide; it is common for a bereaved person to say that he wishes himself dead, and that should not be taken as a cause for serious alarm, but if there is reason to suspect that the person is actively considering suicide, then psychiatric referral is demanded. It is unusual for someone to kill himself without first announcing his intention to at least one other person (the notion that "those who talk about it never do it" is inaccurate and dangerous), and all one usually has to do is ask the direct question to get the direct answer. People sometimes refrain from being this blunt because they are afraid of putting wicked ideas into other folks' heads, but that is nonsense—asking the direct question "is more likely to save a life than to take one" (698).

Sexual Activity

There has been little investigation of the sexual activity
of newly bereaved widows (or widowers), but available
evidence (699) suggests that sexual activity tends to be low,
at least during the first few postbereavement weeks. Some
of these data are based on studies of elderly persons, however, to whom sexual liaisons, because of cultural habituation, would probably be as forbidden after death as before.
No one has thoroughly investigated the idea, though, of
what can be expected of persons who have been raised and
have lived in a time of greater sexual freedom. It is difficult
to imagine the widow dashing from the deathbed to the
dalliance, but that may be what happens; perhaps there is
a "merry widow" syndrome, and in fact at least some bereaved persons probably enter into hyperactive social adventures as a form of denial or of grief avoidance, but the
rate of incidence is unknown. The closest research evidence
at this writing is Pomeroy's finding that widows who have
one "intimate other," such as a lover, and particularly if
the intimate relationship has been one of long duration, will
survive the spouse's death with a relatively optimistic view
of the future and will cope more successfully with their
bereavements than will widows without such intimate
others (700). It seems fairly certain that after several weeks
have passed, if not before, the surviving spouse's sex needs
will reassert themselves at whatever level was normal for
the person before bereavement—or even at some increased
level. The fact is entirely natural, but it is a cause in some
for guilt and overreaction and is difficult socially for many
persons (701). Informal observations suggest that sex problems are particularly acute with older widows and widowers,
many of whom are sexually energetic, but whose sexual
opportunities are carefully monitored by their own puritan-
ical adult children. Even enlightened adults seem to be ap-
palled when they learn that hallowed, widowed Granny
wants now to "live in sin."

MAKING THINGS EASIER FOR FUTURE SURVIVORS

The Will

While he is alive, well, and capable, everyone should, first, have a will drawn by an attorney (so that one's belongings will be disposed of as he wishes and one's family will be cared for as he prefers). Husband and wife should have separate wills, as should any adult children. The person who dies without a will (intestate) presents his survivors with many problems he would probably prefer avoiding for them, and may in fact set up a situation in which his estate will be administered by the state in some slow way which is directly contrary to what he might have desired.

Letter of Instruction

Second, the person should prepare certain information about himself in a "letter of last instructions." This letter should be kept in some convenient place, the location of which is well known to members of the household and to close friends as well, or given to the person who has been selected as executor of one's affairs, with the precautionary note that this particular information should *not* be kept sealed with the will since the will may not be seen until some days after there is need for these more basic data. The data may well be marked and regarded as confidential. Information suggested is basic, and anyone may add as he sees fit; it should be reviewed annually, and updated as necessary, with the date of any changes noted clearly on those changes. The suggestion above is that everyone do this—in families, as observed, this task is not limited to the head of household.

Notification. The person should specify any certain people he wants notified in the event of his death, and provide their telephone numbers and addresses. Family, friends, and particular business associates are clearly among those who might receive immediate notification, along with the person who has been selected as executor or trustee of the estate. Others should probably include the attorney, insurance agents, accountant, banker, investment advisor, physician (this person should be asked to obtain several copies of the death certificate, which will be needed for insurance and other purposes), the personnel office at one's place of employment, the appropriate persons in any fraternal organizations or professional associations, the preferred funeral director and manager of the place where the burial site is situated. It is desirable to notify the children's school counselor, and any person close to the deceased.

Survivor Income. The survivor will need to visit the Social Security office fairly soon after the death, and he will probably want to since there may be a variety of benefits available through that source although maybe not right away. A widow probably will not receive death benefits until she is 60 years old, and if she takes death benefits then rather than at age 62, she will lose a percentage of her total lifetime benefits. Even then, she will receive less than 100% of the benefits her husband would have received had he lived, or half of those benefits (for which he and his employers have paid) if she remarries. The obvious solution, which some widows follow, is to cohabit without benefit of clergy.

The sad fact is that 65% of American widows live below poverty levels, and the average loss in income during the 2 years following bereavement ranges between 44% and 57% (702). These peculiarities in the Social Security system are especially unfortunate when it is recognized that the average age of widows in the United States is only 52 years (703).

Immediate benefits for parents with dependent children can include a percentage of death allowances until the youngest child is 18 years old. It is the time between the youngest child's 18th birthday and the surviving spouse's 60th birthday which tends to be financially critical.

(It is not related directly to these discussions, but perhaps of passing interest to observe that some elderly people are compelled to divorce late in life in order to gain their full Social Security benefits, and surviving widows and widowers who wish to marry are often obliged to live together "in sin," so that their old age benefits will not be reduced below an intolerable level. One must wonder where "sin" really lies, when these kinds of conditions are virtually mandated by circumstance.)

Making contact with the Veterans Administration very soon can be helpful if the deceased had been in the service since burial and headstone rights may be available if they are requested.

Immediate Postbereavement Details. If the individual is a member of a memorial society,* the name of that society should be provided, along with the name of the cooperating mortuary or burial site. A statement should be provided too as to the individual's preference for cremation or burial, or if arrangements have been made for bequeathal. If for some reason the person does not wish to be embalmed, he should say so. Embalming is generally required by law only when the body is to be shipped across a state line, or if it must be preserved for some unusual length of time, or if death resulted from a communicable disease. If the person specifies that he is not to be embalmed, however, he probably should not also ask for an open casket funeral.

If emblaming is to be done, it should be done within 12 hours of death. If the person prefers cremation, he should state his desires in regard to the ashes. (There can be an urn, which may be placed in a niche, buried, or entombed; in some places ashes may be scattered.) Further, if future cremation is preferred, this choice should be cleared with other family members in advance and with their full understanding, as they (or some of them) are the ones who will have to contend with it at the time.

---

*Information regarding memorial societies may be obtained by corresponding with the Continental Association of Funeral and Memorial Societies, 1828 L Street, N.W., Washington, D.C. 20036.

Some persons prefer earth burial, while others want a tomb. If "any old box will do," the person should specify that he wants a cheap pine box; if he does not specify this, the family will probably not provide it since a princely casket may be a provision better suited to their own needs for social conformity, for providing an acceptable send-off, or for expiating their guilt. If survivors have been *instructed* to secure a "pine box," the burden of choice at a difficult time is not necessary. Should the individual wish to devise his own epitaph, arrangements for its engraving should be made in advance and full details provided in the letter of last instructions.

> *In this little urn is laid*
> *Prudence Baldwin (once my maid),*
> *From whose happy spark here let*
> *Spring the purple violet.*
> > *ROBERT HERRICK*

Immediate survivors may not be emotionally capable of remembering basic information concerning the deceased's personal history. Accordingly, he should provide his date and place of birth, the full name of his parents (including his mother's maiden name) and their death dates and places of burial, his Social Security number, and information regarding military service, including any service-connected disabilities. Additional helpful information would include the names and addresses of living relatives.

The person's preferences concerning a service in his memory should be specified—this can save survivors a lot of difficulty. Such services may be conventional (specification as to preference for open or closed casket should be provided) or a more simple memorial service, and either type may be open to friends and relatives, or private, as preferred, and may be conducted at a church, in a funeral home, in a private home, or elsewhere. The individual should specify by name the clergyman or other person whom he wishes to conduct the service (this does not by law have to be some ordained individual) and indicate any music which he would particularly like to have rendered at the service. Some indication should be given as to the limit on money which is to be spent by survivors in memorial activities; the person may, in life, save his survivors large sums if he presents them with definite cash guidelines which he expects them to observe after his death. Obviously, if the individual has purchased a casket and burial plot in advance of need, full information concerning these arrangements (e.g., do they include provision for perpetual care?), together with any related papers, should be included in the letter of last instructions. People commonly want to know if flowers are appropriate at a particular funeral, and if the person has a preference for remembrances of another kind (charity contributions, etc.) he should specify his desires. It is very desirable for persons to work out their funeral and burial arrangements well in advance of need. While funeral directors as a group are no less ethical than members of any other industry, they are in business and they do seek legitimate profit after costs of doing business. Some funeral directors push beyond that which is legitimate in their pursuit of profit, and an emotional and grief-stricken client can be a vulnerable target. Making arrangements in advance solves the problems which may be involved, particularly those relating to prices, options, legal requirements, services to be provided, embalming, and so on. It should be remembered too that funeral and burial are two separate activities, commonly under two separate managements.

> *No wreaths, please—especially no hothouse flowers. Some common memento is better, something he prized and is known by: his old clothes—a few books, perhaps.*
> WILLIAM CARLOS WILLIAMS

The individual should identify the bank in which his safety deposit box is located and indicate the number of that box and where its key is kept. The person should also indicate any contents of his safety deposit box belonging to other persons, and what others have keys to the box. If the individual has any business or personal papers at home, a guide to what is located where should prove very helpful, and if he is self-employed his employer Social Security number is essential.

A statement should be given as to where one's will is located, and if any additions or changes have been made which for some reason have not been filed with the principal will, and the location of the amendment should be provided. Any codicil to one's will should be with the will itself, and it will normally be just as easy to see to that arrangement as it would be to include directions to various parts of the will in one's letter of last instructions. The name and address of the attorney who drew the will should be provided if this information is not clearly indicated on the will itself.

Certain data are required by the funeral director for providing obituary notices to newspapers (which commonly do not accept such notices from unknown persons). The kind of thing newspapers need includes the dates when the person moved to the community, his occupation and place of employment, organizations to which the person belongs, the schools he attended and degrees and honors which were received, dates and places of military service and the armed forces branch. (It is particularly important that veterans provide the dates and places of their enlistment and termination, a copy of separation papers, and a clear notation of the military branch and of the service identification number.)

The date and place of marriage should be given, and the names and birthdates of children, with addresses (and married names of children, when appropriate) should be given. In the event the person was previously married, the name of the former spouse should be provided, with some specification of how the marriage was terminated and where there exists evidence of that termination, together with the names, birthdates, and present addresses of any children of the former marriage.

Financial Data. The person should specify clearly what death benefits are due members of his family via insurance (life, casualty, health), Social Security, Workmen's Compensation, fraternal organizations, unions, Veterans Administration, and the like. The information should be thorough. If the person receives any rents, pensions, or annuities, or if he has benefits under profitsharing or kindred plans, the character of these assets and resources should be described in detail. The location of any records pertaining to such assets should be given. Any debts which the person owes should be noted with full particulars. These would include real estate loans, other loans, charge accounts (with account numbers), and the like. It is particularly desirable to indicate which of these debts are insured so that they would be paid off in the event of death, and important to identify what assets have been used as collateral for loans. If the person has created any trust for any purpose, or if he has some power under another person's trust, details should be provided.

The exact legal description of any owned real estate, or property in which the person has an interest, should be provided, as should data on stocks, bonds (including United States Savings Bonds), mutual funds, debentures, and mortgages. Included with these data should be some estimate from the head of household or the family's financial manager (typically the husband but not necessarily so) as to the worth of the home and what he anticipates will happen to its market value across the next several years. Details of the home's financing should be provided here as well, together with advice concerning an additional postmortem trust deed for raising extra cash, use of insurance to pay off existing loans, etc. The location should be given for papers such as leases, mortgages or other deeds, loans, title and mortgage insurance, and tax receipts.

The person should identify by bank and number any checking accounts or savings accounts which he holds, and if the signatures of any other persons are required to withdraw funds from any such account these persons' names should be given. Should the person have an account with any credit union, savings and loan association, or similar organization, his papers should give full particulars.

Full particulars should be provided regarding any business in which he has an interest, including any interest in the insurance on someone else's life, any debts owed him, any legal matters pending in which he has an interest, and other kindred data which would help others to carry out his financial affairs and to manage them satisfactorily.

A letter of last instructions can be particularly helpful to those who survive a death if its author bears in mind that no one will later understand his personal affairs as well as he does now and prepares his instructions very thoroughly as a means of helping those who live after. Though not a will, the letter can contain small bequests and indicate the person's own preferences concerning disposition of personal items not included in his will; and beyond that, the husband's (or financial manager's) letter should spell out carefully any details concerning the management of household business affairs: what persons in the community have served as gardeners, plumbers, mechanics, tax consultants, how to pay the bills, etc. A wife (or husband) should make no assumptions regarding the spouse's skills in household management and should be as specific as possible in that letter of last instructions about such matters as where to shop for what, where the food is in the house, how the washing machine operates and who fixes it, and so on.

It's an excellent idea for the home's major income provider to have an amount of cash in savings equal to that person's take-home income for at least 2 months, and preferably several more, to provide ready cash during the time between death and settlement of the estate. It should also be anticipated, with whatever planning is desirable in individual cases, that completion of the probate procedure may require from 9 months to over 1 year. It is worth noting too that the settlement of an estate may cost money: there can be fees for lawyers, appraisers, executors, bonds, court, and so on. The savings account should be set up with the bank in such a way that the death survivor can draw on it.

If specific provision has not been made in life insurance policies themselves or in the will, it would be desirable to specify how the person wants his insurance benefits delivered. There are various ways in which this can be managed, and guidance should be sought from a trusted and qualified person as to what is best in particular circumstances. Additionally, it would be well to provide guidance as to how insurance benefits should be invested, given realities of particular situations. Various investment strategies are available for differing needs, ranging from savings accounts in commercial banks, savings and loan institutions, credit unions, and the like, through longterm certificates of deposit, municipal or corporate bonds, and conservative or speculative stocks. The older the survivors are the more conservative their investments should be.

Perhaps there is little that an individual angry citizen can do about a system of Social Security which operates well only for those who are already socially and economically secure, but one can do something about his own pension system if it is defective—he can start by making inquiries about it. The first thing to establish is whether or not one's survivors are entitled to pension benefits, unused vacation pay, and so on. (Why shouldn't they be? The fact that the person who earned these benefits has died is irrelevant; his intent in earning benefits was for the protection of his family as well as himself.) A second question relates to how much entitlement is available to survivors and what, if anything, an employee must do to arrange that such benefits be provided promptly in the event of death. A third question has to do with whether a survivor is entitled to benefits in the event of remarriage; if entitlement stops under such conditions, one may want to know why—again, since the benefits are commonly what he himself has earned and which should be payable as the person who has earned them wishes. Whatever benefits may be available to the survivor should be spelled out in one's letter of last instructions together with specific information as to how those benefits are to be obtained. One should not assume that his company will volunteer anything to his survivors. (The employee who has not been with a company long may not be "vested," and thus his survivors will not enjoy benefits; even under these conditions, however, if the employee has contributed to the retirement program his personal contributions should be recoverable.)

Tips for the Survivor

The letter of last instructions should probably contain some specific warning to the principal survivor to not sign anything unless it is first read by some close, identified friend, or by the family's lawyer or some other trusted individual who is named in the letter of last instructions. The survivor should be warned not to accept any C.O.D. package said to have been ordered by the deceased unless there is clear proof of such an order, not to have the house painted or subjected to new siding (or whatever) unless there is clear proof that the deceased actually ordered the doing of such work. There *are* swindlers around who *do* prey on widows and orphans.

A MATTER OF PROFESSIONAL CONCERN

A special note is in order, at the conclusion, for professional counselors and other trained mental health specialists. If the counselor is immediately involved in a grief situation, particularly if the situation is one in which the counselor's life space is heavily invested in the other person and the reverse is true, the counselor should not try to help others as a professional. He should let himself be the patient. If he is somewhat removed, the counselor can be the professional only in the early crisis if he happens to be there or if he is called in as a friend of the family, but he should withdraw as soon as there is someone else who is competent and work with his own grief. The rule is that the counselor is a professional, and he is supposed to be able to put his own feelings aside from time to time in order to help others, but there are limits on what the counselor can expect of himself and on what others can expect of him. He should not try to be superman—he probably will not be effective. When he finally falls apart he may do damage to the emotional states of others, and if the counselor does not come apart he may damage himself.

The helper is human too.

REFERENCES

1. Ernest Becker, 1973
2. Fulton and Fulton, 1971
3. Hinton, 1966
4. Colin Parkes, 1972, p 98
5. Natterson and Knudson, 1960
6. Friedman et al., 1963
7. Gullo, 1975
8. Parkes, 1972, p 64
9. Fulton and Fulton, 1971
10. See also Schneidman, 1973
11. Glaser and Strauss, 1968
12. Glaser and Strauss, 1965
13. Kubler-Ross, 1970, p 7
14. Jeanne Quint, 1966
15. See also Glaser and Strauss, 1963
16. See also Quint, 1967
17. See also Sudnow, 1967
18. See also Duff and Hollingshead, 1968
19. Kron, 1976
20. See also Heifetz and Nagel, 1975
21. Kubler-Ross, 1970, p 141
22. Kubler-Ross, 1970, p 28
23. Kubler-Ross, 1970, p 36
24. Glaser and Strauss, 1963
25. Kubler-Ross, 1970, p 160
26. Quint, 1966
27. Kubler-Ross, 1970, p 142
28. Kubler-Ross, 1970, p 31
29. Kubler-Ross, 1970, p 141
30. Frances Mervyn, 1971
31. Calkins, 1972
32. Mervyn, 1971
33. Quint, 1966
34. Kubler-Ross, 1970, p 168
35. Kubler-Ross, 1970, p 168
36. See Ball, 1976
37. See Carey, 1977
38. Kubler-Ross, 1970, p 169
39. Kubler-Ross, 1970, p 169
40. Parkes, 1972, p 131
41. Parkes, 1972, p 154
42. Parkes, 1972, p 131
43. Richard Vanden Bergh, 1961
44. See Bonnell, 1971
45. See Reeves et al., 1973
46. See Bane et al., 1975
47. See Arrowsmith, 1975

48. See Jernigan, 1976
49. Verwoerdt, 1968
50. Aldrich, 1962
51. Solnit, 1973
52. Alby and Alby, 1973
53. Spinetto et al., 1974
54. Friedman et al., 1963
55. Fulton and Fulton, 1971
56. Jeanne Quint, 1966
57. Kubler-Ross, 1970, p 115
58. Kubler-Ross, 1970, p 21
59. Glaser and Strauss, 1965, p 33
60. Jo-Eileen Gyulay, 1976
61. See Calkins, 1972
62. Natterson and Knudson, 1960
63. Friedman et al., 1963
64. Stickman and Schoenberg, 1972
65. Parkes, 1972, p 131
66. Kubler-Ross, 1970, p 37
67. Kubler-Ross, 1970, p 270
68. Kubler-Ross, 1970, p 119
69. Kubler-Ross, 1970, p 143
70. Parkes, 1972, p 152
71. See also Sobel, 1969
72. Vanden Bergh, 1966
73. Parkes, 1972, p 152
74. Mervyn, 1971
75. Kubler-Ross, 1970, p 24
76. Fulton and Fulton, 1971
77. Kubler-Ross, 1970, p 39
78. Natterson and Knudson, 1960
79. Freeman et al., 1972
80. Kubler-Ross, 1970, p 39
81. Kubler-Ross, 1970, p 32
82. Kubler-Ross, 1970, p 32
83. Kubler-Ross, 1970, p 39
84. Kubler-Ross, 1970, p 41
85. Kubler-Ross, 1970, p 39
86. Kubler-Ross, 1970, p 41
87. Kubler-Ross, 1970, p 42
88. Kubler-Ross, 1970, p 40
89. Kubler-Ross, 1970, p 159
90. Mauksch, 1975
91. Kubler-Ross, 1970, p 117
92. Kubler-Ross, 1970, p 138
93. Gyulay, 1976
94. Kubler-Ross, 1970, p 140
95. See Calkins, 1972
96. Volkan, 1975
97. Kubler-Ross, 1970, p 112
98. Mauksch, 1975, p 12
99. Kubler-Ross, 1970, p 52
100. See Janken, 1974
101. Mauksch, 1975, p 11
102. Mervyn, 1964
103. Kubler-Ross, 1970, p 52
104. Kubler-Ross, 1970, p 56
105. Kubler-Ross, 1970, p 82
106. Gyulay, 1976
107. Kubler-Ross, 1970, p 83
108. Kubler-Ross, 1970, p 84
109. Kubler-Ross, 1970, p 86
110. Beck, 1967, p 64
111. Kubler-Ross, 1970, p 86
112. See Furman, 1974
113. Weisman and Hackett, 1961
114. Kubler-Ross, 1970, p 88
115. Kubler-Ross, 1970, p 86
116. Kubler-Ross, 1970, p 88
117. Kubler-Ross, 1970, p 86
118. Kubler-Ross, 1970, p 88
119. Lange, 1971
120. Osis and Haraldsson, 1977 p 69; also pp 121, 122
121. Kubler-Ross, 1970, p 112
122. Kubler-Ross, 1970, p 114
123. Fulton and Fulton, 1971
124. Mervyn, 1971
125. Kubler-Ross, 1970, p 113
126. Gyulay, 1976
127. Gyulay, 1976
128. Kubler-Ross, 1970, p 119
129. Kubler-Ross, 1970, p 114
130. Kubler-Ross, 1970, p 120
131. Kubler-Ross, 1970, p 116
132. Kubler-Ross, 1970, p 170
133. Gyulay, 1976
134. Moody, 1976, pp 147, 148

135. Osis, 1961
136. Osis and Haraldsson, 1977
137. Osis and Haraldsson, 1977, p 154
138. Moody, 1976
139. Moody, 1976, p 24
140. Moody, 1976, p 26
141. Moody, 1976, p 30
142. Moody, 1976, p 30
143. Osis and Haraldsson, 1977, p 39
144. Moody, 1976, p 53
145. Moody, 1976, p 57
146. Osis and Haraldsson, 1977, pp 28, 29
147. Osis and Haraldsson, 1977, p 56
148. Osis and Haraldsson, 1977, p 80
149. Osis and Haraldsson, 1977, p 159
150. Osis and Haraldsson, 1977, p 170
151. Osis and Haraldsson, 1977, pp 184, 195
152. Moody, 1976, p 59
153. Osis and Haraldsson, 1977, p 41
154. Osis and Haraldsson, 1977, p 62
155. Moody, 1976, p 64
156. Osis and Haraldsson, 1977, p 190
157. Osis and Haraldsson, 1977, p 24
158. Moody, 1976, p 73
159. Osis and Haraldsson, 1977, p 170
160. Osis and Haraldsson, 1977, p 61
161. Osis and Haraldsson, 1977, p 71
162. Osis and Haraldsson, 1977, p 71
163. See Mendelson, 1974, p 105 ff
164. Westman et al., 1976
165. See Aray, 1973
166. Moss and Moss, 1973
167. See Click, 1973
168. Parkes, 1975b
169. Davis, 1975
170. Carey, 1977
171. Freud, 1917
172. See Lopata, 1975
173. See Salzberger, 1975
174. See Lindemann, 1976
175. Pollock, 1961
176. Salzberger, 1975
177. Prado de Molina, 1976
178. Silverman, 1977
179. Smith, 1975
180. Engel, 1962, p 274
181. Fulton and Fulton, 1971
182. Parkes, 1972, p 6
183. Siggins, 1966
184. Parkes, 1970, 1972, 1973, 1975a, 1975b; also Parkes and Brown, 1972
185. Parkes, 1970
186. Parkes, 1972
187. Parkes, 1972, p 6
188. Fernichel, 1945, p 162
189. Engel, 1964
190. Parkes, 1972, p 10
191. Parkes, 1972, p 5
192. Engel, 1962, p 274
193. Nichols and Nichols, 1975
194. Parkes, 1972, p 5
195. See Parkes, 1972, p 5
196. Parkes, 1972, p 162
197. Parkes, 1972, pp 118, 133; and Parkes, 1975
198. Pollock, 1972
199. Parkes, 1972, p 121
200. Glaser and Strauss, 1965
201. Calkins, 1972
202. Parkes, 1972, p 138
203. Parkes, 1970
204. Parkes, 1970
205. Parkes, 1972, p 138
206. Guthiel, 1966, p 349

207. Engel, 1964
208. Engel, 1962, pp 279–280
209. Bowlby, 1963
210. Nichols and Nichols, 1975, p 95
211. Parkes, 1972, p 123
212. See also Carey, 1977
213. Pomeroy, 1975
214. Fulton and Fulton, 1971
215. Ball, 1976
216. Carey, 1977
217. Fulton and Fulton, 1971
218. Dennell et al., 1970
219. Alby, 1974
220. Seitz and Warrick, 1974
221. Tooley, 1975
222. Gullo, 1975
223. Bowlby, 1963
224. Parkes, 1972, p 120
225. Fulton and Fulton, 1971
226. See also Levin, 1966
227. Schor, 1974
228. Parkes, 1972, p 122
229. Blauner, 1966
230. Parkes, 1972, p 122
231. See Pomeroy, 1975
232. Engel, 1964
233. Blauner, 1966
234. Parkes, 1972, p 123
235. Blauner, 1966
236. Parkes, 1972, p 8
237. Lopata, 1973
238. Parkes, 1972, pp 9, 10
239. Parkes, 1972, p 99
240. See also Schoenberg et al., 1975
241. Parkes, 1972, p 7
242. Pollock, 1961
243. See Silverman, 1977
244. Lopata, 1973
245. Pomeroy, 1975
246. Pomeroy, 1975
247. Parkes, 1972, p 10
248. Gullo, 1975
249. Kubler–Ross, 1970, p 158
250. Blinder, 1972
251. Stein, 1972
252. Mendelson, 1974, p 105 ff
253. Wolfenstein, 1966
254. Burlingham, 1962, p 168
255. See Schoenberg et al., 1975
256. Bowlby, 1967, p 13
257. Nagera, 1970
258. McConville et al., 1970
259. Kubler–Ross, 1970, p 128
260. See Kastenbaum and Aisenberg, 1972
261. Pomerance, 1973
262. Levinson, 1967
263. Anthony, 1940
264. Gartley and Bernasconi, 1967
265. Nagy, 1948
266. Kastenbaum and Aisenberg, 1972
267. Ilg and Ames, 1955
268. Kubler-Ross, 1970, pp 3, 128
269. Kubler–Ross, 1970, p 128
270. Greenberg, 1975
271. Furman, 1973
272. Wolfenstein, 1968
273. Nagera, 1970
274. Moriarty, 1967
275. Furman, 1973
276. Pomerance, 1973
277. Furman, 1964
278. Gyulay, 1975
279. Clay, 1976
280. Nagera, 1970
281. Furman, 1970
282. See also Pomerance, 1973
283. See also Arrowsmith, 1975
284. See also Bane et al., 1975
285. See also Lampl-de Groot, 1976
286. Phipps, 1974, p 22
287. Kubler-Ross, 1970, p 7
288. Brown, 1961
289. Beck, 1967, p 218 ff
290. See also Gregory, 1961
291. See also Birchtnell, 1970

292. See also Atwood, 1974
293. See also Miller, 1974
294. Wolfenstein, 1966
295. Bendiksen, 1975
296. Bendiksen and Fulton, 1975
297. Wolfenstein, 1966
298. Nagera, 1970
299. Atwood, 1974, p 302
300. Kollar and Parsons, 1969, 1973
301. Rochlin, 1963
302. Kubler-Ross, 1970, p 179
303. Mendelson, 1975
304. Blank, 1975
305. Clark, 1972
306. Corwin, 1974
307. Gyulay, 1975
308. Townes et al., 1974
309. Gyulay, 1975
310. Meyers and Pitt, 1976
311. Lindemann, 1944
312. Fulton and Fulton, 1971
313. Fulton and Fulton, 1971
314. Ball, 1976
315. Vachon, 1976
316. Kubler-Ross, 1970, p 275
317. Gyulay, 1975
318. Engel, 1964
319. Gyulay, 1976
320. Parkes, 1972, p 62
321. Townes et al., 1974
322. Friedman et al., 1963
323. Levinson, 1972
324. Parkes, 1972, p 130
325. See also Fulton and Fulton, 1971
326. See also Vollman et al., 1971
327. See also Williams et al., 1972
328. See also Levinson, 1972
329. See also Surawicz, 1973
330. Surawicz, 1973
331. Levinson, 1972
332. Surawicz, 1973
333. Clayton et al., 1973
334. Parkes, 1973
335. See also Skelton and Dominian, 1973
336. Kubler-Ross, 1970, p 159
337. Parkes, 1972, p 62
338. Mauksch, 1975
339. Gyulay, 1975
340. Binger et al., 1969
341. See Kubler-Ross, 1975, p xix
342. Hay and Oken, 1972
343. Mauksch, 1975, p 10
344. Kubler-Ross, 1970, 1975
345. Mauksch, 1975, p 15
346. Mervyn, 1964
347. Mauksch, 1975, p 9
348. Binger et al., 1969
349. Fulton, 1971
350. Natterson and Knudson, 1960
351. Calkins, 1972
352. Gyulay, 1976
353. See also Spitzer and Foltz, 1964
354. See also Mauksch, 1975, pp 11, 14
355. Glaser and Strauss, 1965
356. Holsclaw, 1965
357. Mervyn, 1971
358. See also Bowers, 1964
359. See also Fulton and Langdon, 1964
360. See also Quint, 1967
361. See also Sobel, 1969
362. See also Ford, 1971
363. Calkins, 1972
364. Kubler-Ross, 1970, p 169
365. Kubler-Ross, 1970, p 161
366. Engel, 1964
367. See Stickman and Schoenberg, 1972
368. Kubler-Ross, 1970, p 161
369. Parkes, 1972, p 139
370. Kubler-Ross, 1970, p 162
371. Kubler-Ross, 1970, p 160
372. Gyulay, 1976

373. Kubler-Ross, 1970, p 170
374. See Bonnell, 1971
375. See Reeves et al., 1973
376. See Arrowsmith, 1975
377. See Bane et al., 1975
378. See Jernigan, 1976
379. Engel, 1964
380. Parkes, 1972, p 8
381. Parkes, 1972, p 128
382. Levinson, 1972
383. Fulton and Fulton, 1971
384. Natterson and Knudson, 1960
385. Friedman et al., 1963
386. Fulton and Fulton, 1971
387. See also Vollman et al., 1971
388. See also Levinson, 1972
389. See also Williams et al., 1972
390. See also Surawicz, 1973
391. Pomeroy, 1975
392. Mendelson, 1974, p 121
393. Lopata, 1975
394. Bowlby, 1960
395. Bowlby, 1961
396. Moss and Moss, 1973
397. Parkes, 1972, p 7
398. Parkes, 1972, p 127
399. Parkes, 1972, p 103
400. Kubler-Ross, 1970, p 168
401. Parkes, 1970
402. Prado de Molina, 1976
403. Engel, 1964; see also Engel, 1962, p 274
404. Parkes, 1970; also 1972, p 65
405. Nichols and Nichols, 1975, p 51
406. Barinbaum, 1976
407. Falek and Britton, 1974
408. Lifton, 1967
409. Falek and Britton, 1974
410. Barinbaum, 1976
411. Robson, 1974
412. Gardener and Pritchard, 1977
413. Mitford, 1963
414. Engel, 1962, p 274; also 1964
415. Engel, 1962, p 274; also 1964
416. Parkes, 1972, p 37
417. Parkes, 1970
418. See Parkes, 1972, p 30
419. Parkes, 1972, p 36
420. Parkes, 1972, p 34
421. Gordon, 1975
422. Parkes, 1972, p 81
423. Gyulay, 1975
424. See Reeves et al., 1973
425. See Arrowsmith, 1975
426. See Bane, 1975
427. See Jernigan, 1976
428. Ablon, 1971
429. Engel, 1962, p 279
430. See also Bowlby, 1963
431. Parkes, 1972, p 6
432. Also, see Moss and Moss, 1973
433. Falek and Britton, 1974
434. Engel, 1964
435. Prado de Molina, 1976
436. Parkes, 1970
437. Engel, 1962, p 275
438. Parkes, 1972, p 42
439. Also, see Finichel, 1945
440. Engel, 1964
441. Parkes, 1972, p 53
442. Engel, 1964
443. Engel, 1964
444. Engel, 1964
445. Parkes, 1972, p 41
446. Engel, 1964
447. Engel, 1964
448. Fulton and Fulton, 1971
449. Engel, 1962, p 276; also 1964
450. Engel, 1962, p 279
451. Parkes, 1972, p 39
452. Lindemann, 1944
453. Parkes, 1972, p 39
454. See also Pollock, 1961
455. Parkes, 1972, p 40

456. Mendelson, 1974, p 117
457. Parkes, 1972, pp 39, 40
458. Bowlby, 1963
459. Parkes, 1972, p 67
460. Bowlby, 1961
461. Parkes, 1972, p 73
462. Parkes, 1972, p 46
463. Lindemann, 1944
464. Parkes, 1972, p 73
465. Parkes, 1972, p 56
466. Parkes, 1972, p 40
467. Pollock, 1961
468. Bowlby, 1963
469. Parkes, 1972, p 44
470. Parkes, 1972, p 45
471. Parkes, 1972, pp 44, 45
472. Parkes, 1972, pp 58, 59
473. Parkes, 1972, p 50
474. Parkes, 1972, p 57
475. Rees, 1971
476. Matchett, 1972
477. Parkes, 1972, p 60
478. Lindemann, 1944
479. Engel, 1964
480. Parkes, 1972, p 48
481. Parkes, 1972, p 69
482. See Kubler-Ross, 1970, p 77
483. Parkes, 1972, p 61
484. Parkes, 1972, p 59
485. Parkes, 1972, pp 50, 51
486. See Nichols and Nichols,
     1975, p 91
487. Parkes, 1972, p 51
488. Parkes, 1972, p 52
489. Parkes, 1972, p 50
490. Parkes, 1972, p 53
491. Parkes, 1972, p 60
492. Bowlby, 1961
493. Engel, 1964
494. Pollock, 1975
495. Kubler-Ross, 1970, p 177
496. Kubler-Ross, 1970, p 159
497. Falek and Britton, 1976
498. Parkes, 1972, pp 78, 87
499. Bowlby, 1963
500. Parkes, 1972, p 79

501. Lindemann, 1944
502. Parkes, 1972, p 85
503. Lindemann, 1944
504. Engel, 1964
505. Parkes, 1972, pp 80, 82
506. Parkes, 1972, p 82
507. See Abrams and Finesinger,
     1953
508. See Rothenberg, 1961
509. See Friedman et al., 1963
510. See Berman, 1973, pp 283,
     388
511. See Schuyler, 1973
512. Bowlby, 1961
513. Kubler-Ross, 1970, p 4
514. Bowlby, 1963
515. Parkes, 1972, p 84
516. Mendelson, 1974
517. Stichman and Schoenberg,
     1972
518. Skelton and Dominian, 1973
519. See Bainton and Peterson,
     1961
520. See Rosen and Bibring, 1966
521. See Sonneberg, 1972
522. See Stichman and Schoen-
     berg, 1972
523. See Berman, 1973
524. See Lewis, 1973
525. See Skelton and Dominian,
     1973
526. See Surawicz, 1973
527. See Bruhn et al., 1974
528. Bender, 1954
529. Mendelson, 1974, p 116
530. See also Parkes, 1975a
531. See Schoenberg et al., 1975
     See Sheskin and Wallace,
     1976
533. See Rudestam, 1977
534. Schuyler, 1973
535. Rudestam, 1977
536. Schuyler, 1973
537. Lindemann, 1953
538. Clayton et al., 1971
539. Lindemann, 1944

167

540. Parkes, 1972, p 83
541. Parkes, 1972, p 134
542. Engel, 1964
543. Clayton et al., 1971
544. Kubler-Ross, 1970, p 273
545. Kubler-Ross, 1970, p 4
546. Parkes, 1972, p 85
547. Parkes, 1972, p 79
548. Mendelson, 1974, p 116
549. Anderson, 1949
550. Titchener and Kapp, 1976
551. Degner, 1976
552. Raphael, 1975
553. Clayton et al., 1971
554. For discussion, see
     Mauksch, 1975
555. Townes et al., 1974
556. Mendelson, 1974, p 155
557. Rosenblatt et al., 1972
558. Parkes, 1972, p 82
559. Kubler-Ross, 1970, p 180
560. Bowlby, 1963
561. Parkes, 1972, p 78
562. Falek and Britton, 1974
563. Parkes, 1972, p 87
564. Mendelson, 1974, p 113
565. Parkes, 1970
566. Bowlby, in Parkes, 1972,
     p 94
567. Mendelson, 1974, p 120
568. Clayton et al., 1974
569. Priest and Crisp, 1973
570. Parkes, 1972, pp 79, 94
571. Parkes, 1972, p 107
572. See Guthiel, 1966
573. See Clayton et al., 1974
574. Beck, 1967, p 40
575. Bornstein et al., 1973
576. Clayton et al., 1972
577. Birchtnell, 1970
578. Brown et al., 1977
579. Bunch et al., 1971
580. Lopata, 1975
581. Haberstein and Lamers,
     1963
582. Engel, 1964

583. Engel, 1962, p 278
584. Mendelbaum, 1959
585. Bowlby, 1961
586. Parkes, 1972, p 128
587. Parkes, 1972, p 175
588. Parkes, 1972, p 50
589. Pollock, 1961
590. Parkes, 1972, p 67
591. Parkes, 1972, p 68
592. Parkes, 1972, p 176
593. Parkes, 1972, p 48
594. See also Mushatt and Werby,
     1972
595. Engel, 1962, p 279
596. Parkes, 1972, p 48
597. Engel, 1964
598. Parkes, 1972, p 48
599. Parkes, 1972, p 70
600. Engel, 1962, p 277; also 1964
601. Parkes, 1972, p xiii
602. Parkes, 1972, p 112
603. Parkes, 1972, p 162
604. Parkes, 1972, pp 158, 161
605. Nichols and Nichols, 1975
606. See also Habenstein and
     Lamers, 1963
607. See also Reeves et al., 1973
608. See also Arrowsmith, 1976
609. See also Bane et al., 1975
610. Prado de Molina, 1976
611. Parkes, 1972, p 158
612. Engel, 1964
613. Parkes, 1972, p 142
614. Engel, 1964
615. Engel, 1964
616. Engel, 1964
617. Nichols and Nichols, 1975
618. Nichols and Nichols, 1975
619. Gyulay, 1975
620. Parkes, 1972, p 160
621. Habenstein and Lamers,
     1963
622. Parkes, 1972, p 154
623. Parkes, 1972, p 143
624. Parkes, 1972, p 162
625. Parkes, 1972, p 163

626. Parkes, 1972, p 169
627. Nichols and Nichols, 1975, p 93
628. Reeves et al., 1973
629. Arrowsmith, 1975
630. Jernigan, 1976
631. Pomeroy, 1975
632. Parkes, 1972, p 169
633. Evans, 1975
634. Parkes, 1972, p 169
635. Lopata, 1975
636. Kubler-Ross, 1970, p 177
637. Parkes, 1972, p 163
638. Clayton et al., 1961
639. Parkes, 1972, p 163
640. Parkes, 1972, p 161
641. Parkes, 1972, p 159
642. Nichols and Nichols, 1975, p 91
643. See Parkes, 1972, p 164
644. Parkes, 1972, p 165
645. Kubler-Ross, 1970, p 179
646. Parkes, 1972, p 162
647. Pomeroy, 1975
648. Pomeroy, 1975
649. Parkes, 1972, p 129
650. Ball, 1976
651. Parkes, 1972
652. Gerber et al., 1975
653. Parkes, 1972, p 21
654. Frederick, 1976
655. Miller and Schoenfeld, 1973
656. Carey, 1977
657. Parkes, 1972, p 19
658. Parkes and Brown, 1972
659. Parkes, 1972, p 19
660. Smith, 1975
661. Vollman et al., 1971
662. Williams et al., 1972
663. Calkins, 1972
664. Maddison and Walker, 1967
665. Clayton, 1973
666. Parkes, 1972, p 16
667. Parkes, 1972, p 15
668. See also Kraus and Lilienfield, 1959
669. See also Young et al., 1963
670. See also Cox and Ford, 1964
671. See also Clayton et al., 1968
672. See also Schoenberg et al., 1975
673. Hollister, 1972
674. Patterson, 1972
675. Pradhan, 1972
676. Clayton et al., 1971
677. Pomeroy, 1975
678. Parkes, 1972, p 171
679. Parkes, 1972, p 23
680. Binger et al., 1969
681. Parkes, 1972, p 107
682. Parkes, 1972, p 165
683. Guthiel, 1966
684. Guthiel, p 165
685. Lindemann, 1944
686. Parkes, 1972, p 111
687. Guthiel, 1966
688. Parkes, 1972, p 134
689. See Birtchtnell, 1970
690. See Bunch et al., 1971
691. See Mendelson, 1974, p 133
692. See Brown et al., 1977
693. Parkes, 1972, p 133
694. Parkes, 1972, p 132
695. Lindemann, 1944
696. Parkes, 1972, p 142
697. Parkes, 1972, p 52
698. Parkes, 1972, p 165
699. Parkes, 1972, p 99
700. Pomeroy, 1975
701. See Glick et al., 1974
702. Lewis, 1975
703. Lewis, A. 1975

BIBLIOGRAPHY

Ablon J: Bereavement in a Samoan community. Br J Med Psychol 44:329, 1971

Abraham R, Finesinger J: Guilt reactions in patients with cancer. Cancer 6:474, 1953

Alby N: The replacement child. Evol psychiatr 39:557, 1974

Alby N, Alby J: The Doctor and the Dying Child. In The Child and His Family: The Impact of Disease and Death. Anthony E. Koupelnick C (eds). New York, Wiley, 1973

Aldrich C: The dying patient's grief. JAMA 184:109, 1963

Anderson C: Aspects of pathological grief and mourning. Int J Psychoanal 30:48, 1959

Anthony S: The Child's Discovery of Death. New York, Harcourt-Brace, 1940

Aray J: Unconscious factors in provoked abortions. Alter-Jornal Estudos Psicadinamicos 3:50, 1973

Arieti S: American Handbook of Psychiatry. New York, Basic Books, 1966

Arnstein H: What to Tell Your Child. New York, Bobbs-Merrill, 1962

Arrowsmith F: Pastoral counseling with the dying and bereaved. (Doctoral dissertation, Claremont School of Theology, 1975.) Dissertation Abstracts 36:2993, 1975

171

Atwood G: The loss of a loved parent and the origin of salvation fantasies. Psychotherapy: Theory, Research & Practice 11:256, 1974

Bainton C, Peterson D: Death from coronary heart disease in persons 50 years of age and younger. N Engl J Med 268:569, 1967

Ball J: Widow's grief: The impact of age and mode of death. Omega 7:307, 1976

Bane J, Jutscher A, Neale R, et al. (eds): Death and Ministry: Pastoral Care of the Dying and Bereaved. New York, Seabury, 1975

Barinbaum L: Death of young sons and husbands. Omega 7:171, 1976

Barrett W: Death-bed Visions. London, Methuen, 1926

Beck A: Depression, Causes and Treatment. Philadelphia, University of Pennsylvania Press, 1967

Becker E: The Denial of Death. New York, Free Press, 1973

Bender L: Dynamic Psychopathology of Childhood Vol 2 Children's Reaction—Death of a Sibling, 1954

Bendiksen R: Death and the child: An anterospective test of the childhood bereavement and later behavior disorder hypothesis. (Doctoral Dissertation, University of Minnesota, 1974.) Dissertation Abstracts 35:5549, 1975

Bendiksen R, Fulton R: Death and the child: An anterospective test of the childhood bereavement and later behavior disorder hypothesis. Omega 6:45, 1975

Bermann E: Death terror: Observations of interaction patterns in an American family. Omega 4:275, 1973

Binger C, Albin A. Feurstein R. Kushner J, Zoger S, Mikkelsen C: Childhood leukemia: Emotional impact on patient and family. N Engl J Med 280:414, 1969

Birtchnell J: Depression in relation to early and recent parent death. Br J Psychiatr 116:299, 1970

Blank H: Crisis consultation. Int J Soc Psychiatr 21:179, 1975

Blauner R: Death and the social structure. Psychiatry 25:378, 1966

Blinder B: Child Psychiatry and Human Development. New York, Behavior Publications, 1972

Bonnel G: The pastor's role in counseling the bereaved. Pastoral Psychol 22:27, 1971

Bornstein P, Clayton P, Halikas J, et al: The depression of widowhood after 13 months. Br J Psychiatr 112:561, 1973

Bowers M: Counseling the Dying. New York, Nelson, 1964

Bowlby J: Grief and mourning in infancy and early childhood. Psychoanal Stud Child 15:9, 1960

Bowlby J: Process of mourning. Int J Psychoanal 42:317, 1961

Bowlby J: Pathological mourning and childhood mourning. J Psychoanal Assoc 11:500, 1963

Bowlby J: in E. Grollman (ed), Explaining Death to Children. Boston, Beacon, 1967

Brown F: Depression and childhood bereavement. J Ment Sci 107:754, 1961

Brown G, Harris T, Copeland J: Depression and loss. Br J Psychiatr 130:11, 1977

Bruhn J, Paredes A, Adsett C, Wolf S: Psychological predictions of sudden death in myocardial infarction. J Psychosom Res 18:187, 1974

Bunch J, Barraclough B, Sainsbury P: Suicide following bereavement of parents. Soc Psychiatr 6:193, 1971

Bunch J, Barraclough B, Nelson B, Sainsbury P: Early parental bereavement and suicide. Soc Psychiatr 6:200, 1971

Calkins K: Shouldering a burden. Omega 3:23, 1972

Carey R: The widowed: A year later. J Couns Psychol 24:125, 1977

Clark M: A therapeutic approach to treating a grieving 2½-year-old. J Am Acad Child Psychiatr 11:705, 1972

Clay V: Children deal with death. School Counselor, January, 1976

Clayton P: The clinical morbidity of the first year of bereavement: A review. Comprehens Psychiatr 14:151, 1973

Clayton P, Desmarais L, Winoken G: A study of normal bereavement. Am J Psychiatr 125:168, 1968

Clayton P, Halikas J, Maurice W: The bereavement of the widowed. Dis Nerv Syst 32:597, 1971

Clayton P, Halikas J, Maurice W: The depression of widowhood. Br J Psychiatr 120:71, 1972

Clayton P, Halikas J, Maurice W, Robins E: Anticipating grief and widowhood. Br J Psychiatr 122:47, 1973

Clayton P, Herjanic M, Murphy G, Woodruff R: Mourning and depression: Their similarities and differences. Can Psychiatr Assoc J 19:309, 1974

Click R: The relationship between grief and change. (Doctoral dissertation, Claremont School of Theology, 1973.) Dissertation Abstracts 34:2923, 1973

Cox P, Ford J: The mortality of widows shortly after widowhood. Lancet:163, 1964

Davis S: Grief following loss of kidney function. Aust Occupat Therap J 22:161, 1975

Degner L: Death in disaster: Implications for bereavement. Essence 1:69, 1976

Duff R, Hollingshead A: Sickness and Society. New York, Harper & Row, 1958

Engel G: Psychological Development in Health and Disease. Philadelphia, Saunders, 1962

Engel G: Grief and grieving. Am J Nurs 64:93, 1964

Evans J: Impact of theological orientation on pastors' griefwork therapy with grieving church members. (Doctoral dissertation, California School of Professional Psychology, San Francisco.) Dissertation Abstracts 36:3032, 1975

Falek A, Britton S: Phases in coping: The hypothesis and its implications. Soc Biol 21:1, 1974

Feifel H: Physicians consider death. Proc Am Psychiatr Assoc 2:201, 1967

Fernichel O: The Psychoanalytic Theory of Neurosis. New York, Norton, 1945

Ford K: Dealing with death and dying through family-centered care. Nurs Clin North Am 7:53, 1971

Frederick J: Grief as a disease process. Omega 7:297, 1976

Freeman A, Kaplan H, Sadock B: Modern Synopsis of Comprehensive Textbook of Psychiatry. Baltimore, Williams & Wilkins, 1972

Freud A: Disscussion of Dr. John Bowlby's paper, "Grief and mourning in childhood." Psychoanal Stud Child 15:53, 1960

Freud A, Burlingham D: War and Children. In What to Tell Your Child. Arnstein H (ed). New York, Bobbs-Merill, 1962

Freud S: Mourning and Melancholia. London, Hogarth, 1917

Friedman S, Chodoff P, Mason J, Hamburg D: Behavioral observations on parents anticipating the death of a child. Pediatrics 25:610, 1963

Fulton R, Fulton J: A psychosocial aspect of terminal care: Anticipatory grief. Omega 2:91–100, 1971

Fulton R, Langton P: Attitudes toward death. Nurs Forum 3:105, 1964

Fulton R (ed), with Bendiksen R: Death and Identity. Bowie, Md., Charles Press, 1976

Furman R: Death and the young child. Psychoanal Stud Child 19:321, 377, 1964

Furman R: The Child's Reaction to Death in the Family. In Loss and Grief: Psychological Management in the Medical Practice. Schoenberg E (ed). New York, Columbia University Press, 1970

Furman R: A Child's Capacity to Mourn. In The Child and His Family: The Impact of Disease and Death. Anthony E (ed). New York, Wiley, 1973

Furman R: A Child's Parent Dies. New Haven, Yale University Press, 1973

Gardner A, Pritchard M: Mourning, mummification, and living with the dead. Br J Psychiatr 130:23, 1977

Gartley W, Bernasconi M: The concept of death in children. J Genet Psychol 110:71, 1967.

Gerber I, Rusalem R, Hannon N, Battin D, Arkin A: Anticipatory grief and ages widows and widowers. J Gerontol 30:225, 1975

Glaser B, Strauss A: Awareness of Dying. Chicago, Aldine, 1965

Glaser B, Strauss A: Time for Dying. Chicago, Aldine, 1968

Glick I, Weiss R, Parkes M: The First Year of Bereavement. New York, Wiley, 1974

Gordon A: The Jewish View of Death: Guidelines for Mourning. In Death: The Final Stage of Growth. Kubler–Ross E (ed). New York, Spectrum, 1975

Greenberg L: Therapeutic grief work with children. Social Casework 56:396, 1975

Gregory I: Retrospective data concerning childhood loss of a parent. Arch Gen Psychiatr 15:362, 1966

Grollman E: Explaining Death to Children. Boston, Beacon, 1967

Gullo S: A study of selected psychological, psychosomatic and somatic reactions in women anticipating the death of a husband. (Doctoral dissertation, Columbia University, 1974.) Dissertation Abstracts 35:5113, 1975

Guthiel E: Reactive Depressions. In American Handbook of Psychiatry. Arieti S (ed). New York, Basic Books, 1966

Gyulay J: The forgotten grievers. Am J Nurs 75:1476, 1975

Gyulay J: Care of the dying child. Nurs Clin North Am 11:95, 1976

Habenstein R, Lamers W: Funeral Customs the World Over. Milwaukee, Bulfin, 1963

Hagin R, Corwin C: Bereaved children. J Clin Child Psychol 3:39, 1974

Hay D, Oken D: The psychological stresses of intensive care nursing. Psychosom Med 34:109, 1972

Heifetz M, Mangel C: The Right to Die. New York, Putnam, 1975

Hinton J: Facing death. J Psychosom Res 10:22, 1966

Hollister L: Psychotherapeutic drugs in the dying and bereaved. J Thanatol 2:623, 1972

175

Holsclaw P: Nursing in high emotional risk areas. Nurs Forum 4:36, 1965

Ilg F, Ames I: Child Behavior. New York, Harper, 1955

Janken J: The nurse in crisis. Nurs Clin North Am 9:17, 1972

Jernigan H: Bringing together psychology and theology: reflections on ministry to the bereaved. J Pastoral Care 30:88, 1976

Kastenbaum R, Aisenberg R: The Psychology of Death. New York, Springer, 1972

Kennell J, Slyter H, Klaus M: The mourning response of parents to the death of a newborn infant. N Engl J Med 283:344, 1970

Kollar N: Death and Other Living Things. Dayton, Pflaum/Standard, 1973

Kraus A, Lilienfeld A: Some epidemiologic aspects of the high mortality rate in a young widowed group. J Chron Disabil 10:207, 1959

Kron J: Designing a better place to die. New York 9:43, 1976

Krupp G: The bereavement reaction. Psychoanal Stud Soc 2:42, 1962

Kubler-Ross E: On Death and Dying. New York, Macmillan, 1970

Kubler-Ross E (ed): Death: The Final Stage of Growth. New York, Spectrum, 1975

Kutscher A (ed): Death and Bereavement. Srpingfield, Thomas, 1969

Lampl-de Groot J: Mourning in a 6-year-old girl. Psychoanal Stud Child 31:273, 1976

Lange J: Dying with dignity: Everyone's birthright. Menninger Perspect 2:8, 1971

Levin S: Report of the panel on depression and object loss. J Am Psychoanal Assoc 14:142, 1966

Levinson B: The pet and the child's bereavement. Ment Hyg April, 1967

Levinson P: On sudden death. Psychiatry 35:160, 1972

Lewis A, Burns B: Three Out Of Four Wives: Widowhood in America. New York, Macmillian, 1975

Lewis R: Approach to sudden death outside the hospital. Heart Lung 2:862, 1973

Lifton R: Death in Life. New York, Random House, 1967

Lindemann E: Symptomatology and management of acute grief. Am J Psychiatr 101:141, 1944

Lindemann E: Grief and grief management: Some reflections. J Pastoral Care 30:198, 1976

Linzer N (ed): Understanding Bereavement and Grief. New York, Yeshiva University Press, 1977

Lopata H: Living through widowhood. Psychol Today 7:87, 1973

Lopata H: On widowhood: Grief work and identity reconstruction. J Geriat Psychiatr 8:41, 1975

Maddison D, Walker W: Factors affecting the outcome of conjugal bereavement. Br J Psychiatr 113:1057, 1967

Mandelbaum D: Social Uses of Funeral Rites. In The Meaning of Death. Feifal H (ed). New York, McGraw-Hill, 1959

Matchett W: Repeated hallucinatory experiences as a part of the mourning process among Hopi Indian ·women. Psychiatry (Washington DC) 35:185, 1972

Mauksch H: Becoming a nurse. Ann Am Acad Pol.Soc Sci 346:88, 1963

Mauksch H: The Organizational Context of Dying. In Death: The Final Stage of Growth. Kubler–Ross E (ed). New York, Spectrum, 1975

McConville B, Boag L, Purohit A: Mourning processes in children of varying ages. Can Psychiatr Assoc J 15:253, 1970

Mendelson M: Psychoanalytic Concepts of Depression. New York, Spectrum, 1974

Menzies I: A case study in the function of social systems as a defense against anxiety. Hum Relat 13:95, 1960

Mervyn F: The plight of dying patients in hospitals. Am J Nurs 71:1988, 1971

Meyers J, Pitt N: A consultation approach to help a school cope with the bereavement process. Prof Psychol 7:559, 1976

Miles M: The effect of a small group educational/counseling experience on the attitudes toward death and toward dying patients of nurses who work in high-risk death areas of local hospitals. (Doctoral dissertation, University of Missouri-Kansas City, 1976)

Miller J: The effects of aggressive stimulation upon young adults who have experienced the death of a parent during childhood and adolescence. (Doctoral dissertation, New York University, 1973.) Dissertation Abstracts 35:1055, 1974

Miller S, Schoenfeld L: Grief in the Navajo: Psychodynamics and culture. Int J Soc Psychiatry 19:187, 1973

Mitford J: The American Way of Death. New York, Simon & Shuster, 1963

Moody R: Life After Life. New York, Bantam, 1976

Moriarty D: The Loss of Loved Ones. Springfield, Thomas, 1967

Moss S, Moss M: Separation as a death experience. Child Psychiatr Hum Devel 3:187, 1973

Mushatt C, Werby I: Grief and anniversary reactions in a man of 62. Int J Psychoanal Psychother 1:83. 1972

Nagera M: Children's reactions to the death of important objects. Psychoanal Stud Child 25:360, 1970

Natterson J, Knudson A: Observations concerning fear of death in fatally ill children and their mothers. Psychosom Med 22:456, 1960

Nichols R, Nichols J: Funerals: A Time for Grief and Growth. In Death: The Final Stage of Growth. Kubler-Ross E (ed). New York, Spectrum, 1975

Niven D: The Moon's a Balloon. New York, Putnam, 1972

Osis K: Deathbed Observations of Physicians and Nurses. New York, Parapsychology Foundation, 1961.

Osis K, Haroldsson E: At the Hour of Death. New York, Avon, 1977

Parkes C: The first year of bereavement: A longitudinal study. Psychiatry (Washington DC) 33:444, 1970

Parkes C: Bereavement: Studies of Grief in Adult Life. New York, International Universities Press, 1972

Parkes C: Correspondence. Br J Psychiatr 122:615, 1973

Parkes C: Determinants of outcome following bereavement. Omega 6:303, 1975a

Parkes C: Psychosocial transitions: Comparisons between reactions to loss of a limb and loss of a spouse. Br J Psychiatry 127:204, 1975b

Parkes C, Brown R: Health after bereavement: A controlled study of young Boston widows and widowers. Psychosom Med 34:449, 1972

Patterson P: The use and misuse of psychopharmaceuticals by the pediatrician in the care of the dying child and his family. J Thanatol 2:838, 1972

Phipps J: Death's Single Privacy: Grieving and Personal Growth. New York, Seabury, 1974

Pollock G: Mourning and adaptation. Int J Psychoanal 42:343, 1961

Pollock G: On mourning and anniversaries. Israel Ann Psychiatr Relat Discip 10:9, 1972

Pollock G: On mourning, immortality, and utopia. J Am Psychoanal Assoc 23:334, 1975

Pomerance R: Sibling loss in young adult women. (Doctoral dissertation, Boston University Graduate School, 1973.) Dissertation Abstracts 34:1757, 1973

Pomeroy E: Relationship between mourner characteristics and factors affecting grief work. (Doctoral dissertation, University of Southern California, 1975.) Dissertation Abstracts 36:455, 1975

Pradhan S: Basis for psychopharmacotherapy of the dying and the bereaved. J Thanatol 2:820, 1972

Prado de Molina M: The confrontation with death. Am J Psychoanal 36:267, 1976

Priest R, Crisp A: Bereavement and psychiatric symptoms. Psychother Psychodynam 22:166, 1973

Quint J: Obstacles to helping the dying. Am J Nurs 66: 1568, 1966

Quint J: The Nurse and the Dying Patient. New York, Macmillan, 1967

Raphael B: Crisis and loss: Counseling following a disaster. Ment Health Aust 1:118, 1975

Rees W: The hallucinations of widowhood. Br Med J 4:37, 1971

Reeves R, Neal R, Kutscher A (eds): Pastoral Care of the Dying and Bereaved. New York, Health Sciences Publishing, 1973

Robertson J: Some responses of young children to the loss of maternal care. Nurs Times 49:382, 1953

Robson K: Letters to a dead husband. J Geriat Pychiatr 7:208, 1974

Rochlin G: Griefs and Discontents. Boston; Little, Brown, 1965

Rosen J, Bibring G: Psychological reactions of hospitalized male patients to a heart attack. Psychosom Med 28:808, 1966

Rosenblatt P, Jackson D, Walsh R: Coping with anger and aggression in mourning. Omega 3:271, 1972

Rothenberg A: Psychological problems in terminal cancer management. Cancer 14:1063, 1961

Rudestam K: Physical and psychological responses to suicide in the family. J Consult Clin Psychol 45:162, 1977

Salzberger R: Death: Beliefs, activities and reactions of the bereaved. Hum Context 7:103, 1975

Schneidman E: Deaths of Man. New York; Quadrangle/Times, 1973

Schoenberg G, Gerber I, Wiener A, Kutscher A, Peretz D, Carr A: Bereavement: Its Psychosocial Aspects. New York; Columbia University Press, 1975

Schoenburg B: The Nurse's Education for Death. In Death and Bereavement. Kutscher A (ed). Springfield; Thomas, 1969

Schor A: Acute grief in adulthood: Toward a cognitive model of normal and pathological mourning. (Doctoral dissertation, University of Rhode Island, 1974.) Dissertation Abstracts 35:2447, 1974

Schuyler D: Counseling suicide survivors. Omega 4:313, 1973

Siggins L: Mourning: A critical review of the literature. Int J Psychoanal 47:14, 1966

Silverman P, et al: Helping Each Other in Widowhood. New York, Health Science Publishing, 1974

Silverman P: General Aspects. In Understanding Bereavement and Grief. Linzer N (ed). New York; Yeshiva University Press, 1977

Skelton M, Dominian J: Psychological stress in wives of patients with myocardial infarction. Br Med J 14:101, 1973

Smith W: The desolation of Dido: patterns of depression and death anxiety in the adjustment and adaptation behaviors of a sample of variably aged widows. (Doctoral dissertation, Boston University Graduate School, 1975.) Dissertation Abstracts 36:1933, 1975

Sobel D: Personalization of the coronary care unit. Am J Nurs 69:1439, 1969

Solnit A: Who mourns when a child dies? In The Child and His Family: The Impact of Disease and Death. Anthony E, Koupelnic C (eds). New York; Wiley, 1973

Sonneberg S: A special form of survivor syndrome. Psychoanal Quart 1:58, 1972

Soreff S: The impact of staff suicide on a psychotic inpatient unit. J Nerv Ment Dis 161:130, 1975

Spinetta J, Rigler D, Karon M: Personal space as a measure of the dying child's sense of isolation. J Consult Clin Psychol 42:751, 1974

Spitzer S, Folta J: Death in the hospital. Nurs Forum 3:85, 1964

Stein S: About dying. New York; Danbury, 1974

Seitz P, Warrick L: Perinatal death: The grieving mother. Am J Nurs 74:2028, 1974

Sheskin A, Wallace S: Differing bereavements: Suicide, natural and accidental death. Omega 7:229, 1976

Stichman J, Schoenberg J: Heart wife counselors. Omega 3:155, 1972

Sudnow D: Passing On: The Social Organization of Dying. Englewood Cliffs; Prentice-Hall, 1967

Surawicz F: Psychological aspects of sudden cardiac death. Heart Lung 2:836, 1973

Titchener J, Kapp F: Family and character change at Buffalo Creek. Am J Psychiatr 133:295, 1976

Tooley K: The choice of surviving sibling as "scapegoat" in some cases of maternal bereavement. J Child Psychiatr 16:331, 1975

Townes B, Wold D, Holmes T: Parental adjustment to childhood leukemia. J Psychosom Res 18:9, 1974

Vachon M: Stress reactions to bereavement. Essence 1:23, 1976

Vanden Bergh R: To overcome inhibiting emotions. Am J Nurs 66:71, 1966

Verwoerdt A: Comments on Communication with the Fatally Ill. Omega 2:1:10-11, March 1967

Volkan V: More on re-grief therapy. J Thanatol 3:77, 1975

Vollman R, Gangert A, Ricker L, Williams W: The reactions of family systems to sudden and unexpected death. Omega 2:101, 1971

Weisman A, Hackett T: Predilection to death. Psychosom Med 23:232, 1961

Westman J, Cline D, Swift W, Kramer D: Role of child psychiatry in divorce. Arch Gen Psychiatr 121:289, 1976

Williams W, Polack P, Vollman R: Crisis intervention in acute grief. Omega 3:67, 1972

Wolfenstein M: How is mourning possible? Psychoanal Stud Child 21:93, 1966

Young M, Benjamin B, Wallace C: The mortality of widowers. Lancet 2:545, 1963

INDEX

Page numbers followed by ff indicate a comprehensive discussion of that entry.

  meanings of death in, 61ff
  necessary functions within, 67
Fathers, 77, 78
Fatigue, 26, 142
Fear, 74, 82, 85, 90, 94, 98,
  138, 146
"Fighting to the end," 31, 32
Frustration, 62, 78, 117, 119, 137
Funeral directors, 88, 113, 130,
  131, 143
Funerals, 59, 92, 128ff, 153

G

Grandparents, 77, 78
Grief
  age factors influencing, 59
  anticipatory, 4, 8, 29, 79, 82,
    92
  as affective experience, 51
  as process, 53
  chronic, 123, 145, 147
  definition, 48
  delayed, 56, 59, 61, 116, 138,
    145
  determinants of, 57
  dyssynchronous, 93
  ending of, 132
  expression of, 9, 56, 58
  not an illness, 47
  pangs, 104, 119, 128, 145
  patterns, 58
  potential, 62, 64, 65, 92, 103
  preparatory, 9, 14
  process of, 53ff
  prompt, 56
  psychopathological, 22, 64, 73,
    94, 104, 105, 117–119, 129,
    138, 145ff
  reaction, acute, 4
  reaction, determinants, 56, 82
  reaction in other-than-death
    situations, 48

Grief (continued)
  response to persons in, 55
  similar to a wound, 54, 55
  stages of, 53ff, 70, 91ff, 93
  syndrome, 53
  time dimensions of, 49, 50, 55
  work, 50, 51, 55, 144
Guilt, 5, 14, 25, 60, 62, 72–74,
  76, 78, 82, 85, 86, 88–90,
  92, 93, 95, 103, 111, 113ff,
  119, 145, 146, 149

H

Hair, loss of, 59
Hallucinations, 82, 107, 108,138
Health, physical, 141ff
Helpers, 13, 30, 79, 81, 83, 90,
  99, 102, 112, 118, 125, 127,
  128, 130, 132–138, 139ff,
  145, 148
Hope, 21, 22, 83, 96
Hopelessness, 22, 121
Hospice, 6
Hostility, 26, 82
Husband, 61, 62
Hyperactivity, 100
Hypercathexis, 62, 76
Hypochondriasis. *See* Psycho-
  somatic symptoms.

I

Idealization, 110, 122, 125, 126
Identification phenomenon, 94,
  126
Inadequacy, feelings of, 4, 26,
  121
Income, survivor, 151, 152
Insecurity, 68, 118
Insomnia. *See* Sleep, disturb-
  ances of.

185

Interest, 53, 119, 123
"Invisible shroud," 66
Irritability, 111ff
Isolation, 84, 90, 94, 132, 147

K

Kubler-Ross Syndrome, 16ff

L

Lazarus syndrome, 81, 82
Letter of last instructions, 150ff
Libido, 53, 62, 122
"Life after life," 33ff
Life spaces, 62ff
Loneliness, 64, 68, 90, 118, 132
Love, 53, 68, 70

M

Medical environment, 90
Melancholia, 49, 51, 53
Memorials, 110
Memorial societies, 152
Men, responses of, 61, 68
Merry Widow syndrome, 149
Minimizing, 4, 5, 20, 83
Moody Effect, 37ff, 42–45
Mortality rate, following be-
    reavement, 143
Mothers, 17, 27, 61, 62, 77, 82,
    101, 118, 133, 140, 147
Mourning, 51, 53, 131, 132
Mutilation
  feelings of, 94
  of corpse, 125

N

Near-death experiences, 35ff
"Nervous breakdown," 137,
    138, 142
Notifications, 150
Numbness, 93, 95, 145
Nurses, 5, 8, 11, 12, 14, 16, 22,
    23, 32, 62, 84, 86, 91, 146
Nursing homes, 14, 87

O

Orgasm, nocturnal, 138
Overlooked persons, 77ff

P

Pangs. *See* Grief pangs.
Panic, 98, 142, 146
Parents, 17, 32, 49, 62, 65, 77
  dyssynchronous stages, 93
  stresses between, 112
Perseveration, 98, 146
Pets, 70, 71
Physicians, 10–12, 18–20, 22,
    23, 81, 83–85, 88, 99, 112,
    117, 118, 141, 144, 146
"Pig stage," 23
Pining, 93, 100, 101, 104, 107,
    111, 119
Preparation, 56, 81, 82, 92
Projection, 60, 70, 88, 112, 113,
    117ff
Protest–despair–detachment, 93
Psychiatrists, 11, 12, 117, 148
Psychologists, 10, 12, 25, 52,
    57, 77, 91, 117
Psychopathological grief. *See*
    Grief, psychopathological.